REVELATIONS
Wisdom *from* Beyond the Veil

EMPOWERING INSIGHTS
from the NEAR-DEATH
EXPERIENCE

REV. RICHARD E. WARDEN

Table of Contents

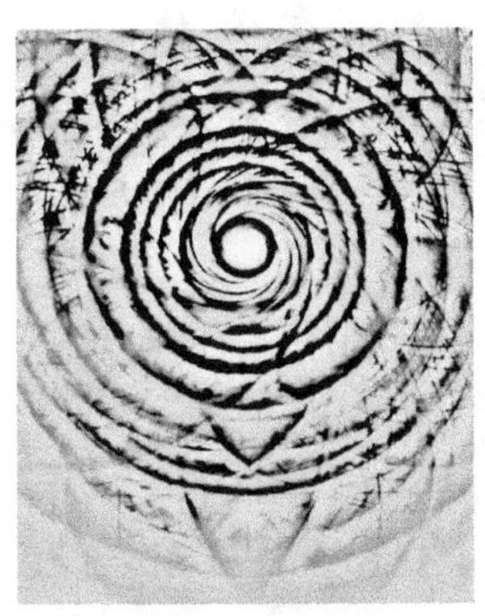

Preface

1978 was a watershed year for me. This was the year I discovered the Near-Death Experience (NDE) when I read Dr. Raymond Moody's book *Life After Life*. Dr. Elisabeth Kubler-Ross' *Death: The Final Stage of Growth* added a new dimension.

In the same year, I also discovered the field of quantum physics when I read Fritjof Capra's *The Tao of Physics* and Gary Zukav's *The Dancing Wu Li Masters*. I also found Itzhak Bentov's *Stalking the Wild Pendulum: On the Mechanics of Consciousness* to be very informative. Written in layman's language, these three books helped focus my growing interest in the laws of nature and how they impact the patterns of human behavior.

Born and raised in rural New York State, I spent my early formative years wandering in woodlands where I observed the reoccurring cycles of life and death. When I read George Storer's *The Web of Life*, what I had seen suddenly made great sense. From that discovery, I developed a keen interest in natural ecological systems and how human activities impact these natural systems. This understanding was helpful when I entered the field of environmental impact analysis years later.

I was a pioneer in the then-emerging field of environmental impact analysis. As such, I helped create some of the initial impact standards. Drawing upon my professional experience, I taught environmental studies at three universities for several years.

My mother was a woman of faith (her family included several Methodist ministers and missionaries), but my father was a skeptic (he believed that many so-called "good Christians" were hypocrites), thus I learned to integrate and balance my intellectual reasoning powers with my intuitive powers of faith in something my mother believed was larger than me. Unable to find a school of theology that taught both reason and faith, in 1996, I found an outlet for my developing beliefs. I was ordained as a priest in the Order of the Melchizedek by the Rev. Dan Chesbro's Church of the Beloved.

From my professional training in environmental impact analysis and my lifelong interest in things theological, I've been trained to "prove it," to substantiate the largely emotional theological suppositions with intellectual "scientific evidence." When I discovered NDEs, this new field held, in my mind, the potential to provide evidence for the existence of a higher power (a deity some call God) and an afterlife. Like many people, I wanted to believe like my mother did but my father's profound skepticism led me to question the unquestioned answers provided by many theological philosophies.

My personal interest in NDEs is grounded in the out of body experience (OBE) I had in 2002. Attempting to make a left-hand turn from a fast-moving country road, my car was struck on the right side. The force of the impact pushed my car sideways down the road 30 feet, causing me to strike my head on the door frame resulting in a contusion. I remember "seeing" the roof of my vehicle disappearing and two black lines extending and converging in the distance ahead of me. I "knew" without words being spoken that if I went there, I would not come back.

I had a choice. Being married to a wonderful lady, enjoying a prosperous life with great prospects for the future, my choice was really a no-brainer. Why choose now to leave? Thus, I know our free will extends well beyond the confines of this earthly plane.

Later, when I discovered the works of the fourth century CE Celtic monk Pelagius, I found a satisfying integration of both my intellectual and intuitive desire to feel a direct connection to God. I find great comfort in his philosophy of the goodness in everything, natural and human. For me, this was my greatest personal surprise, to discover somewhere deep within my soul a direct connection with a higher power, a personal connection with the God Pelagius describes.

For those fellow truth seekers such as myself, I hope that the information I present here opens your mind to the greater truths that are now being revealed by the millions of NDE witnesses.

The supposition of my book is that our human family finds itself in a great spiritual crossroads. We been given a marvelous divine gift; modern medical technological ability to resuscitate the clinically dead. The result has produced millions of near-death experience witnesses who are now providing fascinating and reassuring insights into the nature of an afterlife and a Being of Light many call God.

I believe we have been given this gift at this time due to our rising consciousness of the challenges humankind now faces from global climate changes. There are some who even say if we do not change our current global energy policies, we may self-extinct by 2050.

What many NDE witnesses report is, in my opinion, very uplifting and encouraging. Adding to that the ecologically aware religious philosophy of Pelagius and his fellow early British Christians, I find great hope for the future.

I also strongly believe in Divine Guidance; when I have a question, the answer quickly appears. The latest example was when I was looking for a picture for this book that expresses its metaphysical nature, I came upon a vendor stall at our local Renaissance Festival. There, I saw a painting entitled *The Vortex* by John Sosnowsky. It immediately "spoke" to me. I asked for, and was quickly granted by John, permission to use it. Truly, there are no accidents in the universe!

The fact that you have picked up and are reading this book also confirms to me that there are no accidents in philosophy. I hope you find what you read within these pages enlightening and encouraging. Peace be with you.

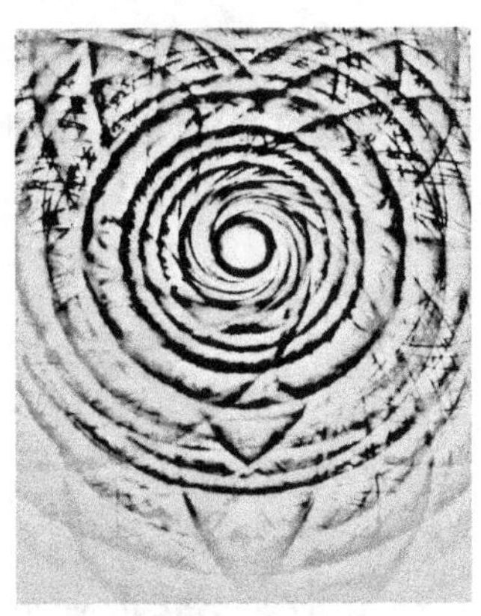

Acknowledgments

I first wish to knowledge the patient caring support of my publisher, Michelle Kulp. She has the patience of Job. After patiently waiting for four years, divine guidance told us both it was time to quit writing and get it published!

Similarly, the long years of friendship and support from my editor, Juanita Ruth One, has been invaluable in producing the final version of my manuscript.

The insights, humor and great wisdom of my soul brother the Rev. Bil Holton, as we walk the journey of life together, has been invaluable beyond words. Together, with his wife Rev. Cher Holton, we have enjoyed many long invigorating discussions of things spiritual over the past several years as we learn lessons from our current incarnation in this great cosmic Skin School.

Ben Henry, for his friendship, patience and insights in providing invaluable technical support for this "technologically challenged" author.

John Sosnowsky, artist and enlightened being, for permitting use of his painting Vortex for the cover of this book.

Most of all, I wish to acknowledge the love, support, patience and insights of my soulmate Liz (Lady Liz'Beth) Clickner. We both share a great passion for education and the development of our spiritual growth. We enjoy our marvelous loving journey through life together. Words cannot express the deep love I hold for my Lady Liz'Beth.

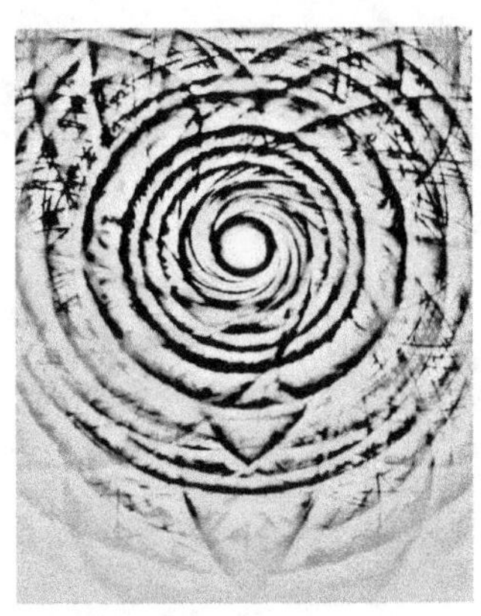

Testimonial

Very succinctly written with compelling, evidence-based research, the author explains how Near Death Experiences can awaken humankind to the truth of its transcendental nature and its collective ability to heal and enlighten – resuscitate – those on the planet who have neglected or forgotten their divine genealogy. It is a must read.

– Rev. Dr. Bil Holton, Co-founder,
The Global Center For Spiritual Awakening

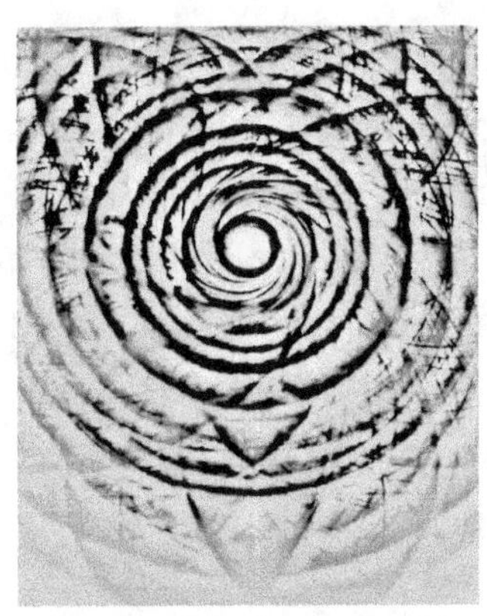

Foreword

I died on December 22, 1964. That was the same day that my daughter, Natalie (meaning child of Christmas), made her entrance into life on Planet Earth. But while the healthy 8 lb. 4 oz baby was lustily adjusting to the bright environment outside of the cozy, dark womb, her mother was dying in a morass of post-partum neglect. I was in a teaching hospital, so the same person never examined me twice. The task of checking on the new mom revolved through a parade of interns, nurses, nurse practitioners, and others.

So, as each one massaged my abdomen and changed the bloody linen, no one realized that this routine stimulating of the uterus to return to pre-birth size was actually causing some internal stitching to burst open. My screams were interpreted as just hysteria and they even moved me to a private room because my behavior was distressing other new moms.

No one, other than my husband, suspected that anything might be wrong. When he expressed concern, the nurses assured him that I was just having a negative reaction to the drugs I had received during labor to which some people react with hysterics. Besides, he was only a first-year medical student, so who was going to listen to him? Eventually, he decided to phone my doctor whom he reached while on a dinner date. In response, my doctor said he would phone the nurse's station for an update then come to the hospital as soon as he finished dining.

Meanwhile, I'd had enough of the gut-wrenching pain and chose to withdraw from the body. My consciousness flew up into a corner of the room from which vantage point I could observe all that was happening. I was delighted to realize that I *still existed* as an aware, thinking entity, no longer the occupant of the tormented body bedded below!

Not only could I watch what was happening, but my hearing also became so acute that I could hear a friend consoling my mother in the waiting room, my husband in the hallway calling his Methodist-minister father to request prayers, and the nurses in the nurses' station lamenting the bother that I had become.

When my doctor arrived, I watched the energy in the room shift into a TV drama. Shocked at seeing a near-lifeless body (my husband said I was as white as the sheets), he yelled for assistance, threw the body on a gurney and raced down the corridors bursting through swinging double doors in a rush to get to an operating room. I followed, flying above the drama below me. As we passed the nurses' station, one exclaimed, "Oh my God, she really was in trouble. She's not going to make it!"

By the time the body was placed on the operating table, I was bored with the entire drama and decided to leave. After all, it was no longer me! So, my consciousness flew out through the top of the hospital into space. I watched as the city of New Orleans rapidly shrank from view and the earth I was departing became a multi-colored blue ball. Most NDErs speak of passing through a tunnel. My take on the tunnel is that in an open field on a clear summer night, the dark starry sky looks like an inverted bowl. If two such bowls were joined, they could create the illusion of a roundness through which one might pass. This was my sensation as I sped out into the darkness of space, but I never sensed any constriction such as a tunnel.

My environment was not unlike the images on TV's *Star Trek* when the Starship Enterprise enters warp speed and a mass of lighted objects go whizzing by. Feeling absolutely elated at having left the heaviness of the suffering painful body, I felt no sense of loss - just elation - finally understanding the true meaning of "free spirit." Suddenly, I noticed a distant bright light unlike anything whizzing past me. I instinctively knew that this was where I had come from and I couldn't wait to return. So I sped up, experiencing what one might call a "quickening of the spirit!"

Approaching the light, I was grateful that I was no longer in a physical body. The light was so brilliant and powerful that I knew, had I still been embodied, it would have instantly blinded, if not vaporized, me! Yet, the light beckoned with such warmth that I could completely understand moths and other insects flying headlong into bright lights.

So, I joyously flew right into the center of the light. Once engulfed in the light, I became aware that I was surrounded by other beings. I felt no fear, just curiosity, questioning, "What are these? Angels or ghosts?" I didn't recognize any departed loved ones nor any recognizable religious figures. However, the beings did have bodies consisting only of light, similar to the space aliens in the movie "Cocoon."

As they encircled me, I felt bathed in unconditional love and realized that they were there to welcome and support me! As soon as I acknowledged their presence, they telepathically told me that I had given birth to a little girl back on planet Earth. This was news to me, although I'm sure someone had told me; however, because of the altered state of awareness induced by the drugs given me against my will during labor and then the postpartum-hemorrhage trauma, the news had not registered.

Instantly, it was as if someone placed a strip of neon at my feet and I intuitively knew that I had a choice to make. I could step across that line and remain in this realm of light, with no pain and bathed in unconditional love, OR I could return to planet Earth to take care of my newborn baby. The beings assured me that there was no judgment whatsoever, that whatever I chose to do would be perfectly OK. Needless to say, I chose to return and immediately felt myself being noisily whooshed through a dark tunnel only to awaken in the recovery room, once again weighed down in a pain-filled body.

1964 was before the publication of Dr. Elizabeth Kubler Ross's iconic *Death and Dying* book and prior to Dr. Raymond Moody's active research into the Near-Death Experience. I feared that if I were to tell anyone about what I had just experienced, the next stop would probably have been the psychiatric ward. So, I gave myself amnesia, completely erasing the experience from my memory!

However, 14 years later, while attending a conference at the Edgar Casey Institute in Virginia Beach, serendipity urged me to have my palm read. I was astounded as this psychic affirmed things about my life that no one had a reason to know. Then he said, "When you gave birth to your first daughter, you died and went to the other side." Immediately, the amnesic veil lifted and the entire experience came rushing back in vivid emotional detail.

I am very grateful for the NDE because I no longer live in fear of death. In fact, there are times when, having the honor of being with another human as they passed through that doorway, I have felt envy and longing to return "home." However, thanks to my decision, the surgery and 8½ pints of donated blood, I did return to life and am still here. This tells me that my time has not yet come and that I must still have some work to do here on planet Earth before I can finally go back home. Interestingly enough, that daughter has been one of my greatest teachers in this lifetime and now serves as the Executive Director of her county's Hospice Program.

– Rev. Juanita Ruth One

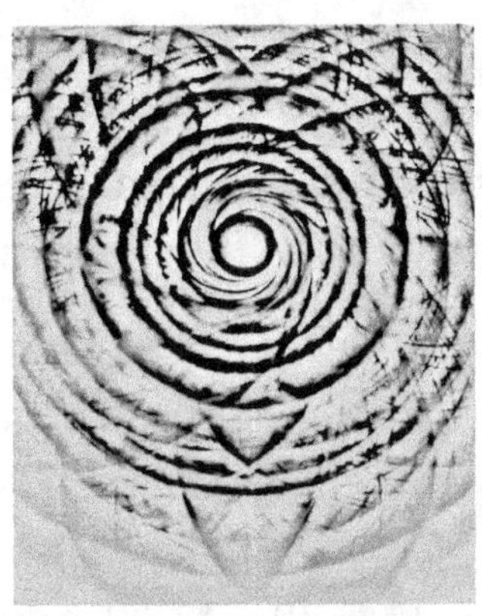

Introduction

I am a spiritual warrior. I seek the truth, ancient or modern, in all religious and scientific experiences, and once I find them, I pursue them with vigor. I seek them motivated by my passion as an educator (Latin root – *educere*, "to lead out, draw out.")

In 1978, I discovered quantum physics and the Near-Death Experience. When I added these two disciplines to my love of history, I developed a belief that the patterns of human behavior are based upon, and reflective of, the laws of nature. In the birth and death cycle of the stars, the rise and the fall of human civilizations, and "for those who have eyes to see," the patterns of our individual lives; I see an eternal flow of uniting energy. Thus, it is in the understanding of the natural laws and human patterns that we begin to understand our personal place in the universe, and in so doing, achieve our ultimate spiritual growth.

A Great Gift

Humankind has been given a great gift from God/Ultimate Reality (i.e., the One Source). It's a Divine Gift, a miracle of modern scientific technology.

Our new medical technologies have *empowered humankind* with the ability to resuscitate the "clinically dead." According to a June 23, 2014 article in *The Epoch Times*, approximately 5% of the US population (13 million) had experienced an NDE in 1992. The article goes on to say that 774 NDEs are experienced in the United States each day. By 2014, this amounted to almost 19 million (about 282,576 per year). At this rate, by the end of 2019, more than 20 million Americans will have come back with wisdom and insights from "the other side."

Collectively, these witnesses are survivors of the *Near-Death Experience* (NDE). What many of them saw and reported back is both *good empowering news* and *not-so-good alarming news*. What I find heartening is what I report in *the best news response to the challenge* section. There is great hope that we may in fact avoid the most serious consequences now being projected.

Because many witnesses reported dire predictions for the future, it seems to me that this modern medical technology is a Divine Gift from an omnibenevolent loving God warning humankind of potential disasters that may lead to our self-extinction if we don't change our current course of events.

Spiritual Crossroads

This is a book of empowering news about eternal truths and a global challenge, a serious warning of potential self-extinction revealed by witnesses who have seen *beyond the veil,* and our increasingly powerful response to the challenge.

From what I have seen, many people, especially our youth, are responding in powerfully meaningful ways that will change the world profoundly.

I believe God/The One Source is urging us to use our innate power of unconditional love to create a future which preserves humankind and the world in which we live.

Book Organization

The Good News – Reassuring and Revealing. This section details what the witnesses saw from beyond the veil. I present some of the ancient wisdom brought forth by a number of the survivors of the near-death experience.

The Challenging News – An Alarming Wake-Up Call. This section describes the *global climate crisis* challenges the witnesses saw and includes current supporting data.

The Great News – a Powerful Response to the Challenge. It appears that our generation of young adults has taken up the climate change challenge and are beginning to make real progress in addressing the challenge. They see the world our generations are leaving them now, are not happy about it, and are taking actions to reverse the trend towards human self-extinction.

Additionally, major world players like Microsoft founder Bill Gates and Britain's Prince Harry have joined in the effort to confront and capitalize on the challenges of climate change.

Supporting Research. After the previous three informative sections, I present some supporting research.

A Joyous Journey. For those readers not familiar with the NDE dynamic, I set forth a generalized overview of the most common elements of the near-death experience including what many believed to be scientific evidence for this metaphysical process.

Aftereffects. I provide a brief overview of the physiological and psychological impacts NDE witnesses have experienced.

Scientific Evidence. A brief review of some of scientific evidence supporting the near-death experience.

Quantum Physics. Science affirms our co-creative power from the God/One Source.

Perennial Principles. The five principles I believe NDE survivors have been witness to.

Genius Masterminds. I invite you to have **Some Serious Fun!** It is my intent to create a **Genius Masterminds Group**— a gathering of researchers dedicated to finding solutions to the global challenge. As a multi-generational team, they will jointly apply the trans-disciplinary power of **Combinatorial Creativity** in both serious and humorous ways.

Appendix—The Diamond Principle of Ethical Reciprocity. This is my modern version of the religious Golden/Silver Rule with which I combine the secular Ethic of Reciprocity. As carbon is the basis of life on earth, I see this as being a Diamond Principle. From my viewpoint, this is as close as humans have come to creating a universal law of mutually beneficial behavior.

The Good News –
Reassuring and Revealing

For millennia, beginning back in pre-civilization eras, humankind has sought answers to the great mysteries of life. Cave art and graves of persons interred 40,000 years ago with sacred objects give testimony to this ancient search for these answers; all in pursuit of satisfaction of *our two basic needs*: safety in the short-term and security in the long-term.

Studies of the collective experiences of these witnesses provide evidence, proof, and testimony to the existence of realms and entities "beyond the veil."

Gifts of Knowledge from NDE witnesses

Drawing upon the vast NDE database created by Kevin Williams and his www.near-death.com website and related internet sources, I present a brief review of some of the very encouraging (a little not so) wisdom reported from a wide spectrum of NDE survivors. To get a more in-depth look at any of the topics presented here, I encourage you to do your own additional in-depth exploration of any of the gifts of knowledge presented herein.

The Nature of Light

The element of light is perhaps the most important element of the near-death experience. Some people have interpreted the light as a Being of Light who radiated love and warmth.

Christians see the light as being represented by Christ. Atheists, on the other hand, may simply see The Light as a shimmering energy that serves us as a guide to the realms of the afterlife.

This is the infinite benevolent eternal creative force of the universe some people call God. Numerous Holy books refer to God in terms of light.

Light has two natures: wave-like (energy) and particle-like (matter) expressed in the form of electromagnetism. This dualistic characteristic of light expresses in the electrons of atoms (negatively charged) that attract and the proton (positively charged) that dissipates; they engage in a sort of cosmic dance of creation.

This interaction produces creative tension that attracts and creates matter and expels and dissipates matter; an eternal dance between the feminine Yin and the masculine Yang forces that produces a third entity (1+1 = 3). The dance is the famous Unity of Opposites.

Physicists tell us the speed of light is constant for all observers. Although how it accomplishes this is not fully known; it does appear that light is the cornerstone of modern physics and natural law.

Photons (a quantum of light particle) vibrate (like the strings of a guitar) and experience resonant frequency (vibrate together).

This explains in scientific terms what happened when God said, "Let there be light, " and there was light. This is how the whole of creation began. The world of science calls this moment "The Big Bang."

Further, physicists discovered that light particles (photons) are entangled and can communicate with one another instantly over vast reaches of space. Beings of Light have this telepathic capability.

God

As noted previously, many people have reported meeting a Being of Light, a single entity that expressed unconditional love for them, and also meeting other Light Beings. As a result, many believed that they had met God and Angels.

In contrast to the traditional Abrahamic religious view of a revengeful God, NDErs commonly see **a new** (or perhaps the original) **version of God.** This God is pure love, appears as energy or Light that can appear in any shape, is unconditionally loving, infinitely forgiving, compassionate, non-judgmental, neither male nor female, infinite, a part of everything that exists, which grants and respects our free will.

Personally, I prefer the term "One Source." Like the laws of nature, it is a neutral all-encompassing term that respects both genders and all philosophical heritages, religious and secular.

To me, God/One Source is darkness and light, energy and matter, expressed as being:

- omnibenevolent (all-loving)

- omnipresent (all-pervading)

- omniscient (all-knowing)

- omnipotent (all-powerful) the **All** in the **All That Is**

Delightfully, some of these witnesses reported that **God has a sense of humor.** David Sunfellow, author of *New Heaven, New Earth,* in his October 23, 2019 issue of *The Formula for Creating Heaven on Earth* presented a few examples.

John K. discovered God has a personality possessed with a sense of humor. God laughed at the thought of this survivor questioning His existence. The survivor realized that he was the shadow and God was the reality.

Leonard reported that communication on the other side is done by telepathy (thought transfer) and that God has a fantastic sense of humor. He was told that life on earth is a big drama and it should not be taken too much in earnest.

Terri E. reported talking directly with Jesus and that he, too, has a wonderful sense of humor. The experiencer distinctly got the feeling that God enjoys us humans in the same way a father enjoys watching the minor scrapes His children get themselves into.

Odell H. also reported Jesus has a sense of humor. Together they laughed at scenes where something funny occurred in his life.

George E. said that God is a great joker, reminding him that he, God, is always with us, that He acts in the everyday world.

One remarkable report spoke of the sound of soft, benevolent laughter which felt like the wise and gentle smile of the Buddha. The voice said, "My child, you must not take things so seriously. You are just part of an evolutionary chain, in which all life evolves in stages of development. You're only human. You need not judge yourself so harshly. Be gentle with yourself."

A woman reported said the Light has an indescribably beautiful smile, an incredible sense of humor and an infectious laugh, that the Light knew her better than she herself and loved her to her core. It found the seriousness with which she viewed herself quite amusing, and that, in the end, her life would be redemptive in a sense that it would ultimately end in love.

As we live our lives in this earthly plane, we must remember simply to laugh and enjoy life, learn not to take ourselves so seriously. On this more advanced plane, these witnesses experienced the joy of knowing they truly are one with the universe.

As the famed French philosopher Voltaire once observed, "God is a comedian playing to an audience who is afraid to laugh."

If you want to read the whole 66 pages of God's humor, visit the-formula.org/heavenly-humor/

Afterlife Realms

Many sources, ancient and modern, believe there are *10 or more* afterlife realms. *Quantum physicists*, using Superstring Theory, theorize a cosmology consisting of 10 dimensions, as did the ancient Greek mathematician *Pythagoras* (who many believe to be the first great mathematician).

Jewish mystics believed the entire creation of the universe is composed of 10 *emanations of light* from 10 *utterances of God*, a perfect order of 10 composed of a hierarchy of 10 angelic realms revealed in the laws of the 10 Commandments.

Buddhists believe there are 10 levels of realization toward enlightenment via the 10 directions of the Buddha's light to the 10 Buddha-realms. *Christian Gnostic's* profess a belief in a cosmology of 10 heavens, as do *Muslims*. The *Judeo-Christian Bible* describes a hierarchy of 10 celestial powers. The famed psychic Edgar Casey believed that our solar system has 10 major spheres (the Sun plus the 9 planets). NDE experiencers Lynnclaire Dennis, Dr. George Ritchie, Betty Eadie, and Swedish scientist Emmanuel Swedenborg also reported multiple levels in the afterlife.

Visually, I found *Figure 30: Interpreting Levels of Life and Consciousness*, a large, full-color teaching poster included inside the back cover of the book **After We Die, What Then?** by George W. Meek, to be one of the most informative presentations of the realms anyone has yet developed. It was published in 1979 by the Metascience Corporation.

If you can obtain a copy of this rather rare book, it may prove very useful in your understanding of the realms of the afterlife. It is presented in five parts.

Part One deals with the true nature and structure of both the human body and the worlds in which it functions.

Part Two deals with 11 types of evidence of survival after physical death.

Part Three contains detailed descriptions of the interpenetrating planes of existence.

Part Four provides answers to 50 specific questions about the system. This includes the proven path for individual soul development (which agrees with the perennial philosophy and the core teachings of all the great religious founders).

Part Five delves into examples of communication with the dead via electronic instrumentation, the main focus of his research.

The Void

Many survivor testimonies involve the experiencer encountering a phenomenon commonly known in NDE circles as "the void," a realm of complete and total darkness – empty of anything except the thought and emotional patterns of those who enter it.

For some, it is a beautiful and heavenly realm where they are able to perfectly see the love and light within themselves. For others, who were temporarily unable to see the love and light within themselves, "the void" was a terrifying, confusing and horrible hellish-like place.

Love does not exist in the void, nor does light. However, escape is always possible. Love, the Light, your faith, guidance from Beings of Light (Angels), or reincarnation can set you free from "the void." All you need to do is ask for help.

Heaven

Many who have survived a near-death experience report that heaven is a state of mind, a condition of the heart. It is neither up above nor down below, but here on earth.

We create our own heavenly or hellish conditions through our belief systems. This is why many NDEers caution us to choose our heavenly realm wisely. Our realm of experience in the afterlife will be based entirely upon *how much we love or do not love* in this lifetime. That's why it is important to learn to "treat, or do not treat others as you would, or would not, be treated, in any given situation."

Hell

Like heaven, hell is a state of mind which acts as a "timeout," a place for reflection, education and purification of negative thought patterns. It is not a place for judgment or punishment; the good news is that it is not an eternal place.

People remain there as long as necessary to serve their spiritual development. It sounds very much like the Christian Roman Catholic belief in *purgatory*. Your Soul will stay there only as long as you need to extract yourself from some strong earthly fixation. Thankfully for most souls, hell is only temporary – not eternally damned.

There are *two realms of hell*; the first is the one we see on earth which is merely a reflection of the inner hell within us as a human being. This hellish state of mind is the result of living a hellish life. The other is the traditional images of hell; the famed fire and brimstone. This one is the result of having either earthly desires that can't be satisfied or by lack of spiritual growth.

Perhaps the most famous description of this realm is from the Christian Bible's Book of Revelation. Although the author cannot be definitively established, what he/she describes is very much like the unpleasant NDEs some people report having witnessed. Apparently, the experience was so frightening to one witness that it figuratively "scared the living hell out of his soul" and so impressed the author that, upon returning, he described the very alarming experience to warn others to behave themselves: practice the love of God, others and yourself or you're certainly going to "go to hell!"

It may well be that many of the prophets from the ancient holy books were survivors of near-death experiences or NDE-like encounters such as reported by Edgar Cayce (the famed Sleeping Prophet).

Religion

Many NDEers report that *love is the true "religion,"* and that while organized religion is not as important as many people believe, religions do have an important purpose. Ancient NDE revelations may, in fact, be the source of many religious concepts.

Some religious beliefs can be harmful, such as soul sleep, (our souls sleep until the resurrection), strict religious fundamentalism (those who employ fear to motivate and control their fellow human beings), religious bigotry (only we have the one true path), extremely faulty religious doctrines, and atheism (under certain conditions).

Spirituality

God is love. Love is supreme. Love is the true "religion!" The earth is a school for learning love. God engages in tough love. (There are no accidents; everything happens for a beneficial purpose. It is through the "Traumas of the Dramas" in our life that we gain our greatest gifts of wisdom.) Love gives us unlimited opportunities to grow spiritually. The spirit of the heart lives on in the afterlife.

Soul and Spirit

Humans are multidimensional beings composed of an unconscious mind (our body's autonomic systems), a subconscious mind (the soul), a conscious mind (the personality, self-consciousness), and a super-conscious mind (the spirit). NDEs reveal our soul's astronomical interconnections. Our multi-dimensional physical body is connected to soul and spirit.

Suicide

Dr. Kenneth Ring, author of *Life at Death* published in 1980, has done extensive research on the topic of suicide. He reports that many people mistakenly believe that suicide is a one-way ticket to hell. This is often traced to faulty religious dogma or cultural influences. There are many ways to commit suicide; for instances, indulging in a long-term junk food habit, lifelong tobacco smoking, drug addiction, and the like.

The consensus seems to be that NDEs reveal that it is *how we live our current life* which determines the quality of life after death, not by how we die.

The special consequences of suicide are no different than other ways of dying; however, there are penalties for hurting others. This is why people considering suicide must understand (if they are emotionally able) why they wish to end their life, prepare themselves for it, and consider the impact that their action may have on others.

Overall, the bottom line must be concern for a person's right to control their own life and death. Persons facing intractable pain or indignities in the final stages of life must have the right to determine for themselves whether life is no longer worth living. The issue of a person's right-to-die is basically a matter of personal liberty, autonomy, equality, dignity, and the right to end unnecessary suffering.

Dr. Ring's Research strongly suggests that the suicide-related NDEs *do not reach completion*; instead, they tend to simply fade out before the characteristics of a non-suicide-related NDE make their appearance. Generally, they did not experience the tunnel, see a brilliant comforting light, see loved ones who died, or enter a world of heavenly beauty. Instead, it seems to end with a feeling of confusion, drifting in a dark or murky place–"the void" described earlier.

They seem to have learned that suicide is not the answer, that while they experience a brief release of pain, there are no long-term benefits.

On a positive note, having entered the great void, some survivors report they found hope there and that this place can be a place of healing. They briefly experience the greater reality of love and light. If they reach out to the beings of light nearby, escape from the avoid as possible.

Atheists

Atheism is not a one-way journey or a surefire track to hell as some religious people contend. The fact is that God cares very little about a person's religion or non-religion. The only thing that matters is the spiritual condition of their heart. When many atheists say they don't believe in God, it's usually the Christian God that they are rejecting. For them, the laws of nature may simply be another form of intelligent design. They may in fact hold beliefs closer to spirituality than religion. Indeed, some atheists found that their NDE profoundly changed their beliefs about the idea of an afterlife.

It's only the spiritual condition of the heart that matters, the motives for their actions. Some atheists discovered at their NDE profoundly change their beliefs about the existence of an afterlife.

Reincarnation

Dr. Ian Stevenson in his 1967 book entitled *Twenty Cases Suggestive of Reincarnation* provides rigorous scientific reasoning for which reincarnation is the only viable explanation that fits the facts of his study. He describes 20 cases of young children who were spontaneously able to describe a previous lifetime as soon as they learned to talk.

Earth

Life on Earth is a "school of hard knocks." God does not give us anything that we cannot handle.

The earth expresses our larger self while our divinity provides a stairway to heaven (Jacob's ladder?) The evolutionary nature of spiritual existence provides support for the concept of evolution (the physical aspect of the metaphysical concept of reincarnation).

As an educator by passion, I believe we are here to learn lessons from a vast Cosmic Curriculum. We select the lesson we wish to learn prior to each incarnation. Our Ego is our test administrator who reveals our lessons in the repeating patterns our behavior; those situations and persons who continue to show up in our life over and over, until we learn the lesson, get the gift of knowledge and go on with our lives.

Most importantly, it is from the "traumas of the dramas" of our life that reveal the major lessons we signed up for in our present enrollment in God's "school of hard knocks."

In my life, it was a loss of sight in my left eye at the age of 16 that presented me with my first major lesson. I learned two things. First, you can beat your head against the wall all you want (stay in a state of denial) but all you get for your efforts is a bloody head. Second, and most important, I learned that *life goes on*. Get the gift of wisdom and incorporate it into your individual wisdom base.

Life in General

Life is about giving, loving and helping others; receiving from God, knowing that Life is God. Life is about us, for the living, and is like a river to travel and enjoy. It's *a school of higher education*, a cycle through which we progress. It was planned by us before our birth.

Upon physical death, we experience a life review, receive a sort of a spiritual *report card* revealing to us what we learned and did not learn in our current life, and are given an opportunity to make whatever corrections are needed to advance the education of our soul.

The Purpose of Life

One consistent aspect of the NDE experience is a *life review*. Often, when looking back at their life, many report feeling profound remorse, along with extreme regret, for the harm that they have done and cannot undo. At the same time, the typical NDEer reports feelings consistent with unconditional love from the Light, which communicates forgiveness because they were still learning how to become a more loving person. Therefore, many tend to say that *learning how to love* is the purpose of life. (Love may contain many more descriptive words like tolerance, humility, letting everything be, trust in God, and the like.)

In other words, the purpose of life is to become more God-like; *to love and forgive unconditionally, with compassion for all*. This should be reassuring to those who suffer from a form of anxiety called *Thanatophobia*, characterized by *fearing one's own death* or the process of dying. As these witnesses affirm, **there is nothing to fear!**

Having experience the beauty and the joy of the afterlife realm many call heaven, some even regretted having to come back to this earthly plane and all of its challenges.

Our Ego

Several witnesses noted our Ego is alive and well after returning from an NDE. They warned readers to be cautious about healers who claim to have healing powers granted to them based on their NDE experience. This has gotten a number of them into some serious ethical problems when what they preached outwardly and lived inwardly proved to be directly contrary to one another.

Personally, I see the Ego as simply our test administrator who presents us with the lessons we have chosen to learn in this lifetime. As an educator, I hold to a radically different point of view from the Ego as a negative influence. I see the God, the One Source, as being a benevolent creator. Our Ego is an extension of this creative source. As such, our Ego is patient and loving. We co-create our world, our Ego is our test administrator testing us to see how well we've learned the lessons we chosen to learn.

Know Thyself

As a number of the healers discovered, knowing our shallow issues (i.e., the limitations that block us from experiencing our full potential) is as important as knowing the beauty, peace, and joy of existence on the other side of the veil. Our motives are as important as our actions. As the ancient Greeks wrote over the entrance of the Temple of Apollo at Delphi these words, "Know thyself and thou shalt know all the mysteries of the gods in the universe."

The Power of Prayer

Perhaps the most important empowering aspect of being human is to experience the *power of prayer;* individual and global. ***The Power of Prayer*** published July 5, 2019 and written by David Sunfellow, administrator of *The Formula for Creating Heaven on Earth* organization cited earlier, states that, "Near-death experiencers champion prayer as a superpower. Along with meditation (feeling the Presence of God), feeling and expressing gratitude, cultivating a sense of humor (which includes not taking ourselves too seriously), and learning how to see things from higher perspectives, near-death experiences indicate that prayer can produce miracles."

Sunfellow cites several articles on the topic.

Pray to God, by Howard Storm from his book *"My Descent Into Death: A Second Chance of Life,"* describes how he discovered how to pray while experiencing a horrendous afterlife situation. Being surrounded by unconditional love profoundly changed his life for the better.

Prayers Gave Me Energy by Dr. Eben Alexander in his book *"Proof of Heaven."* During his traumatic experience, Eben came to realize that hierarchies of beings stretching out into the dark above and below were praying for him. These beings knew he was undergoing a transition, and they were singing and praying to help him keep up his spirits.

Prayer Beams That Felt Like Splashes of Love from her book, *"We Live Forever"* by P.M.H. Atwater. She describes how children could actually see the prayers being said for them and how the power of those prayers turned into beams of radiant gold or rainbow light.

I found *The World Could Be Saved by Prayer Groups* by NDEr Ned Dougherty of particular interest. "I was told that the world could be saved, not by its leaders, but by prayer groups throughout the world. I was told that the prayers of a group of 20 could save a nation from war. I was told that the fate of mankind rested upon our ability, individually and collectively, to change the direction of mankind in accordance with God's plan."

I encourage you to read the full accounts Mr. Sunfellow offered which can be found at:
www.the-formula.org/the-power-of-prayer/

While one person can change the world, prayer groups throughout the world focused on a specific challenge can make a huge change. Just think what power might be generated by global groups focusing on finding solutions to specific challenges like climate change!

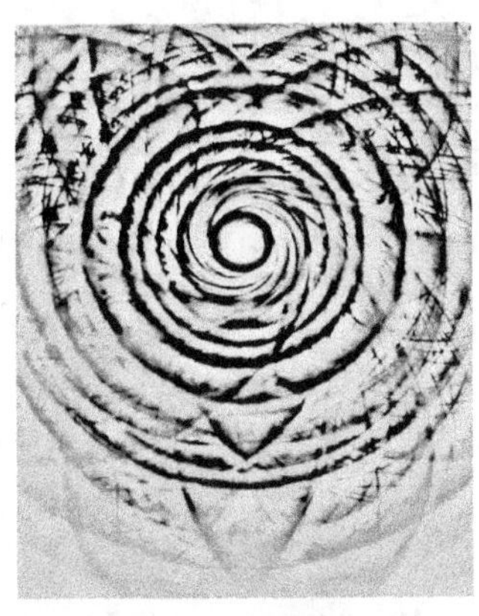

Challenging News –
An Alarming Wake Up Call

Many of these witnesses tell us that the earth and human civilization are at a historic turning point.

Many NDE survivors reported receiving visions of a future in which occur *catastrophic natural disasters*, such as an increase in the strength and frequency of major hurricanes and cyclones.

Long-scale forecasting of *increased hurricane and cyclone* activities do seem to be playing out now. A study published by the Geophysical Physical Dynamics Laboratory (May 31, 2019) entitled *Global Warming and Hurricanes* concluded, in part, that the sea level rise is very likely due to a substantial human contribution to rising global temperatures. Tropical cyclone rainfall rates will likely increase, and the global proportion of tropical cyclones that reach very intense (Category 4 and 5) levels will also likely increase.

Global Ice-Field Melting

There seems to be emerging evidence that these catastrophic predictions may have some validity. Indeed, climate studies over the past couple of decades indicate that the world climate is changing as human activities warm the atmosphere leading to increased global ice field melting resulting in a rise in oceanic sea levels. Recent studies show *Greenland's Ice Sheet is Melting Faster Than We Thought and Shows No Sign of Stopping; the thawing will continue for decades*. (Popular Science, April 23, 2019). One example, August 1, 2019, 12.5 billions of Greenland's ice-sheet melted in just 24 hours.

At the South Pole, things are not much better. A report published by lifescience.com states that *Nearly 25% of West Antarctic Ice is in Danger of Collapse* (May 21, 2019).

Additionally, *In the Himalayas, glacial melting has doubled since 2000, says a new study*. https://www.dailykos.com/ stories/2019/6/24/1866961/-In-the-Himalayas-glacier-melting-has-doubled-since-2000-says-new-study (June 6, 2019).

This latter study says that glaciers in the Himalayas have been losing more than a vertical *foot and a half of ice each year* since 2000 which is *double* the amount of melting that took place from 1975 to 2000. Sometimes called "The Third Pole," the Himalayan Plateau (which includes Mount Everest) is the source of 12 major rivers draining into both the Indian and Pacific oceans (The South China Sea). People who live in Pakistan, Bangladesh, China, India, Nepal, Bhutan, Vietnam, Laos, and Burma (nearly half the world's total population) depend on these water sources for energy, drinking water, and agricultural purposes.

Ocean Circulation

Of more dire concern is the impact of ice-sheet melting that Greenland and the Himalayas have on *ocean circulation.* In the North Atlantic, we have a giant oceanic conveyor belt that brings warm water from the equator north past the east coast of the United States and Canada, past the southern tip of Greenland, eastward to the British Isles and Scandinavia, and southward back to the equator. Cold melt water from Greenland's ice sheet is cooling the water, slowing it down. Eventually this slowing may lead to a cooling of Western Europe and increased heating in eastern United States and Canada.

Similarly, the loss of the Himalayan glaciers would disrupt the convection currents the South China Sea that drive the annual monsoons across Southeast Asia. If the monsoon seasons are shortened, it could lead to widespread crop failure. If Southeast Asia goes barren, all the people in and beyond the region may starve. Just imagine the impact that would have on the already-growing worldwide number of *climate refugees.*

Additionally, the northern part of the *Pacific Ocean* is also being challenged. A November 12, 2019 article in the *Washington Post* entitled "The climate change reaction that threatens the heart of the Pacific" by Simon Denyer and Chris Mooney focused on the collapse of the salmon catch off Japan's northern coast. It has plummeted about 70% in the past 15 years. The drop in production seems to coincide with the loss of sea ice in the Sea of Okhotsk which is wedged between Siberia and Japan. The authors report that in the area some places the temperatures have risen by as much as 3°C since pre-industrial times resulting in it being one of the fastest warming spots in the world, according to data from a nonprofit organization Berkeley Earth. This rapid increase exceeds the policy limits of 2°C set in Paris in 2015.

What is alarming about this is that these rising temperatures are starting to shut down the single most dynamic ice factory on earth. This area generates more ice than any other single place in the Arctic Ocean or Antarctica. Additionally, the sea ice reaches a lower latitude than in any other place on the earth. As they report, "Its decline as a cascade of consequences well beyond Japan as climate dominoes begin to fall. When sea ice forms here, it expels huge amounts of salt in the frigid water below the surface, creating some of the densest ocean water on earth. That water then sinks and travels east, carrying oxygen, iron and other key nutrients into the northern Pacific Ocean, where marine life depends on it.

"As the ice retreats, that nutrient-rich current is weakening, endangering the biological health of the vast northern Pacific– one of the most startling, and least discussed, effects of climate change so far observed. We call the Sea of Okhotsk the heart of the North Pacific," said Kay Ohshima, a polar ocean-ographer at the Institute of Low Temperature Science at Hokkaido University. "But the Sea of Okhotsk is significantly warming, three times faster than the global mean. That causes the power of the heart to weaken."

The article goes on to state that "the cascade starts more than a thousand miles away in a uniquely frigid area of Siberia known as the 'Cold Pole,' where the coldest temperatures ever recorded in the northern hemisphere (-67.7°C) was measured in 1933." However, 'the Cold Pole,' is also warming rapidly by about 2.6°C since pre-industrial times in the village of Oymyakon. That means the bitter north wind that blows down onto the Sea of Okhotsk is also warming."

The warmer winds inhibits the formation of sea ice cover that has shrunk by nearly 30% in the past four decades, a vanishing of about 130,000 square miles of ice (an area larger than the state of Arizona).

The total result of all this is a drastic drop in salmon. Fisherman records show a drop of between 21 and 36 million tons per day in 2012 to a meager 6 tons per day in 2018.

The implications of all of this on the world's food supply is quite obvious.

Boreal Forest and Peat Fires

More recently, in 2019, reports of widespread *forest and peat fires* in the far-northern boreal forests, triggered by lightning from thunderstorms in Siberia, Alaska, northern Canada, and Greenland, have alarmed many of the world's scientists. According to an article entitled *Peat, the world's largest terrestrial carbon store, ignites into "unprecedented" Arctic firestorm,* scientists have never seen anything like this before. The Arctic is warming faster than the rest of the world and the loss of sea ice helped create the tinderbox.

Peat is carbon-rich soil which has grown in cold, moist, and waterlogged environments for thousands of years. However, higher temperatures and drought, due to emissions from fossil fuels, lower the water table making the bogs susceptible to combustion. Once they are ignited, they are almost impossible to extinguish.

https://www.dailykos.com/stories/2019/7/27/1874542/-Peat-the-world-s-largest-terrestrial-carbon-store-ignites-into-unprecedented-Arctic-firestorms

Peat is the world's largest carbon store, holding an estimated CO_2 twice the amount of the current global CO_2 reserves. Just imagine if you can the impact this would have if current world CO_2 levels tripled!

Burning of Amazon Rainforest

Often erroneously called "the lungs of the planet," Public Radio International notes that the Amazon rainforest "absorbed as much CO_2 pollution every year as the amount produced by all the cars on the planet." Further, "deforestation and climate change are pushing the force to a tipping point beyond which it will actually release more CO_2 into the atmosphere than it captures."

Reaching that tipping point would be a significant step backwards in the fight to maintain a healthy climate. Due to rising global temperatures, the Amazon is progressively becoming hotter and drier. This rise is due to significant human behavior such as intentionally setting fires that raises the fuel in this backward loop in three ways.

First, fire destroys trees that release massive amounts of carbon dioxide directly into the atmosphere, accelerating climate change and further drying out the forest.

Second, the fires remove whatever plants are most crucial to carbon sinks. The Amazon ecosystem is one of the world's most important photosynthesis sites. Losing it further dries out the Amazon, increasing the frequency of natural fires.

Third is the issue of transpiration. The roots of trees absorb water from the ground and release it into the air as water vapor. This process forms clouds that transport the water onto other parts of the rainforest, basically creating a self-sustaining system.

This crucial part of the Amazon ecosystem releases up to 20 billion metric tons of water each day. The forest carries more water than the Amazon River, the largest river in the world. The less water released through transpiration, the dryer the entire ecosystem becomes, creating conditions favorable for entirely different habitat: a savanna. As Harvard professor and Amazon researcher Brian Farrell describes, "If fire removes the plant life responsible for moving water up into the clouds, the land will dry and rain forest will be replaced by grasslands able to withstand the newly arid conditions, which persist for thousands of years."

In terms of numbers, leading scientists believe that Amazon could undo this feedback loop if as little as 20% or 25% of the forest is lost. Brazilian government estimates that already 17% of land necessary has been lost already. We could be just a few percentage points of clearing a way for triggering this disastrous feedback loop. For more information, read

www.climaterealityproject.org/blog/why-protecting-amazon-critical-solving-climate-crisis.

Forbes Magazine cited a report released by the National Oceanic and Space Administration (NASA) in August 2019 that noted, "According to Brazil's space research center INPE, almost 73,000 fires have been recorded so far this year. INPE is seeing an 83% increase over the same period in 2018."

To give a bit of perspective, Rhett Butler, a writer at the *Rainforest.mongabay.com* website, wrote in 2012, "Low-level fires in the rain forest are not unusual. Even in 'virgin' forests, fires may burn across thousands of acres of forest during dry years. The distinction between these fires and the fires that the forests are increasingly experiencing today is the frequency of occurrence and level of intensity. Natural fires in the Amazon generally do little more than burn dry leaf litter and small seedlings. Typically these fires have flames that only reach a few inches in height and have virtually no impact on tall trees or the canopy itself."

National Geographic Explorer-at-large ecologist Thomas Lovejoy told Sarah Gibbens in another article (08/22/2019) on *NationalGeographic.com*, "This is without question one of only two times that there have been fires like this in the Amazon… There is no question that this is a consequence of the recent uptick in deforestation."

In another article by Forbes magazine (8-26-19) *It's not just Brazil; Satellites Show Fires Across Bolivia's Amazon and in Central Africa, too,* shows that while the majority of the rain forest is in Brazil, it extends into eight other countries as well, including Bolivia. The joint NASA/NOAA Soumi National Polar-orbiting Partnership (Soumi-NPP) satellite captured images of fires burning in the Bolivian Amazon. Additionally, according to NASA's Fire Information for Resource Management System, sub-Sahara Africa is on fire now, too.

Traditional slash and burn farming techniques where farmers cut down some vegetation and set fire to the rest is a cheap way to clear the land. It is also a troubling technique which leads to deforestation, soil erosion, and biodiversity loss. Rainforests also release carbon dioxide, a greenhouse gas, into the atmosphere. This means these bigger and more frequent fires increasingly make more of a contribution to climate change.

Clearly then, this has been the result of deliberate human behavioral changes. Deliberately clearing away highly productive natural rainforest for the purpose of increasing human agricultural production (in itself an important human goal) has a significant counter-productive result. Reaching a mutually beneficial balance between these two important goals is now crucial to the preservation of the human species.

North Pole Shift

Another projected global challenge is *a shift of the earth's northern magnetic pole* which will cause the mantle of the earth to shift, setting off major new volcanic eruptions.

From fossil records, it is known that the Earth's poles last flipped about 700,000 years ago; a total of 183 times in the last 83 million years.

Because it generally takes as long as a century to achieve this, fears of an imminent pole shift are unfounded and nothing to worry about.

However, in the short run, it has been known that, since the 1800s the magnetic north pole tends to waver. In the following century, the rate of movement increased from nine miles to about 35 miles each year, moving quickly away from Canada, even crossing the international dateline. From 1831 to the late 1940s, scientists discovered that it moved 250 miles to the northwest. *Since 1990, it has moved* an astonishing *600 miles* towards Siberia and is now in the middle of the Arctic Ocean, four degrees south of geographic north, *and still moving.*

Because of its rapid movement, this has led to a major redefining of the World Magnetic Model. On Monday, February 5, 2019, the magnetic model was officially updated noting that the location of the North Pole had changed. Due to the fact that the world's GPS systems depend on an accurate location of the pole, everything from airline routes down to the GPS on your cell phone depends upon this accuracy.

Collapse of the US Federal Government

Yet another projected catastrophic event is *the collapse of the US federal government* which will set off a massive worldwide depression causing major global social upheavals.

While the American political scene is indeed increasingly divided, there seems to be little evidence of an imminent lapse of the federal government.

However, the global trend towards the **rise of authoritarianism** at the expense of democracy is of greater concern to me. We now have more than *one-half of the world's population* living under authoritarian rule.

China, Russia, North Korea, Syria, and Iran are ruled by dictatorial regimes. Others like India, Indonesia, Brazil, Turkey, Italy, Hungary, and the United States see rising tides of conservatism which resists change. As the laws of physics tell us, change is the only constant. Energy is always creating new structures. Nature's basic dynamic is one of progressing forward. Those that resist change eventually are overcome by the relentless progressive dynamic of change. "Time and tide wait for no man," (Geoffrey Chaucer. 14th Century English poet.)

The overall question is: *Does humankind have enough time to alter the tides of climate change to save us from our journey towards self-extinction?*

The severity of this challenge was recently set forth by a paper published in April 2019 by Australia's *Breakthrough National Centre for Climate Restoration* entitled "Climate Crisis Could Bring the End of Human Civilization by 2050…and that's just the start."

The authors believe that the climate crisis is an *existential threat* to human civilization as a whole, our human species, and life on earth. The earth itself will be adversely affected by increased levels of extreme weather events that are bringing record hurricanes, floods, fires, droughts, and related costs to the world economy. It has generated climate refugees, not on just island nations, but in flooded cities along damaged coasts. *You can read more at:* www.breakthroughonline.org.au/papers

On a brighter side, not all studies agree with the gloom and doom projections. A study by the Met Office of United Kingdom published in the Journal *Nature Geoscience* (Sept. 2017), reports that a combination of *three factors* may actually avoid the catastrophic disasters cited above. The new research found that an astonishingly rapid increase in *renewable energy* technologies, a *faster-than-expected reduction* in carbon emissions, and a *slower-than-expected warming* means the world could realistically meet the highly ambitious targets of the 2016 Paris climate agreements to keep global warming to "well below"

2°C above the pre-industrial average, aspiring to keep it below 1.5°C.

They found that what should be a 1.3°C increase above the mid-19th century average is actually about 0.9 to 1°C. While this may not sound like much, it is actually the difference between having 3-to-5 years versus 20 years to reduce emissions to zero. They further suggest that if emissions peak and then drop back below current levels by 2030 and continue to drop more steeply after that, we have about a 66% chance of staying below 1.5°C.

China is Leading the Way

The driving force underlying the above more optimistic climate change forecasts is the role of China. It has the world's largest population and is the second-largest world economic power. Recent studies have shown that China is already affected by worsened floods, more extreme droughts, diminished fish reproduction and other ecological changes. The government has understood for a long time that the warming climate threatens the country's agricultural production, makes economically-important cities subject to catastrophic flooding and that eventually many of the country's rivers may dry up.

The government understands that China faces major water scarcity and that, in the future, this may become worse as much river flow is fed primarily by melt-water which may sharply decrease towards the end of the 21st-century. (See the above article on the increasing melt-water of Himalayan plateau). As a result, the government of China took a giant leap forward when it launched its national carbon market in December 2017. Initially, the national carbon market will cover the power sector, representing about 1,700 mostly state-owned companies that are responsible for roughly one-third of China's total carbon emissions (3.5 billion metric tons, making it the world's largest carbon market).

After 2020, the market is expected to gradually expand to cover 7,000 companies and eight industrial sectors (power, petrochemical, chemical, building materials, iron and steel, nonferrous metals, paper production, and aviation). This eight-sector market would encompass about 9% of 2017 global emissions, exceeding the current world total of all global market systems and raise the share of global emissions covered by carbon pricing to at least 21%. (Read *Why China is at the Center of Our Climate Strategy.* www.edf.org/climate). With China projected to soon be the world's biggest economy leading the way, how long will it be before the rest of the world's economies follow?

Middle East Conflicts

Some witnesses reported seeing *events that may lead to wars* in the Middle East, perhaps even World War III.

Conflicts of religious philosophy have long been considered a major cause of civil conflict and wars. Religious and civil inquisitions have claimed the lives of uncounted tens of thousands of lives.

Events in the Middle East over the past half century or more would seem to alarmingly confirm this possibility. With the discovery of oil in 1898 by the British, followed by the demise of the Ottoman Empire, establishment of the British Mandate, the creation of the Jewish state of Israel and the rise of nationalism in Arab lands, we are witnessing a major clash of economic and religious interests in the Middle East. Economic interests are devoted to full exploration and exploitation of the world's second-largest reserves of oil. Their short-term fossil fuel interest focus is on materialism, while the interests of the religious sector focus is on long-term spiritualism. Add military nuclear weapons capabilities and you have a recipe for disaster.

By recognizing these two driving forces, we can see the great impact human activities are having on the global climate conditions cited above. Only by recognizing legitimate needs and interests of all parties and individuals can we begin to devise effective programs to lessen the negative impacts while there is still time to act.

Soul Pollution

In my opinion, what we human beings are dealing with is *soul pollution*. We are all aware, to at least some degree, that our air, water, and food supplies are being polluted by human actions. I believe its roots are deeper; soul deep, in fact.

Quantum physics tells us everything is energy (in the form of light) and that energy is manifested as matter. Thoughts are energy. Expressed initially from experiences which begin in our mother's womb, we begin to be informed about the world around us. This information (in-form-ation process) begins to program our thoughts in the form of our emotions (e-motion, energy-in-motion). These emotions become ingrained in our *subconscious*. Beneath this, we have all of the autonomic systems (respiratory, digestive, reproductive, etc.) that pre-program our physical reality, forming a basic *unconscious* level of awareness. This is strongly based in the epigenetic programming in our DNA which we inherited from our ancestors.

Post-birth,we begin to learn about the world around us; forming a rudimentary *conscious* level; our mental understanding of the world in which we live. We grow to see the world primarily from a materialistic point of view and thus invest our energies basically in acquiring material wealth.

The social-economic and religious (or nonreligious) circumstances into which we are born continues to influence our conscious understanding of the world around us.

Overlaying all of this conditioning is the ancient wisdom acquired over many millennia of existence, manifested in the super-conscious level.

Thus, we exist in four levels: autonomic-physical, sub-conscious-emotional, conscious-mental, and super-conscious-spiritual; the latter being the abode of our soul. The most powerful of these is the super-conscious level from which I believe the NDE survivors draw their experiences.

Much of the world's physical pollution comes from the pollution of our subconscious and rudimentary mental levels. Our subconscious level is rooted primarily in fear and the mental levels in acquiring material wealth. Unless we consciously begin to access the ancient wisdom of the super-conscious level, we will continue to pollute and destroy the earthly home we have inherited from our ancestors.

This current generation may be the *first* one to recognize these trends, both natural and human, and may be the *last* generation able to do anything about it. We must become consciously aware of the legacy we are leaving our children and grandchildren, and make whatever decisions necessary to change the disruptive course of our current history.

The warning is that if we don't get our act together on the global warming effects of climate change and the current trends against democracy, *we are toast!*

As I said before, I believe humankind is at a great spiritual crossroads. If we do not abandon the use of destructive technology and self-centered destructive policies and actions, our very existence as a species is at stake; we may self-extinct.

Armageddon?

Many NDE witnesses note that if these catastrophes occur, *perhaps two-thirds* of the human population will die. The remaining one-third may then enter into a new era of global peace and enlightenment lasting perhaps a thousand years. From what they described, these apocalyptic visions may occur in this century, resembling, coincidentally, some of the prophecies of the Bible, Edgar Cayce, Nostradamus, the Virgin Mary, visitations of Fatima, and others.

A Message of Empowered Hope

My message of *empowered hope* is that we have been given, at this crucial crossroad in history (as noted above), medical technology that allows us to resuscitate the "clinically dead." In so doing, we now have millions of NDErs who have made us aware that our future, and that of our planet, is now in our hands. The vast majority of witnesses have revealed the existence of a loving, forgiving, and compassionate God/One

Source/Ultimate Reality and the existence of many wondrous realms of an afterlife.

We needn't repeat the errors of our past. To avoid them, we must first be aware that these challenges exist and then respond with effective measures.

To rephrase the well-known quote by the famed Spanish philosopher George Santayana, "Those who do not remember *or know the* past *are* condemned to repeat it."

Overall, what these witnesses report gives me great hope for a peaceful, productive future for our species, preserving the beauty and productivity of our global home. In fact, we may be seeing the beginning of a new epoch, a new **Great Awakening**, both religiously and scientifically. If we don't awaken, the remaining one-third of humanity may be holding a "wake" for the other two-thirds lost to the drastic changes in global climate change.

We live in exciting times!

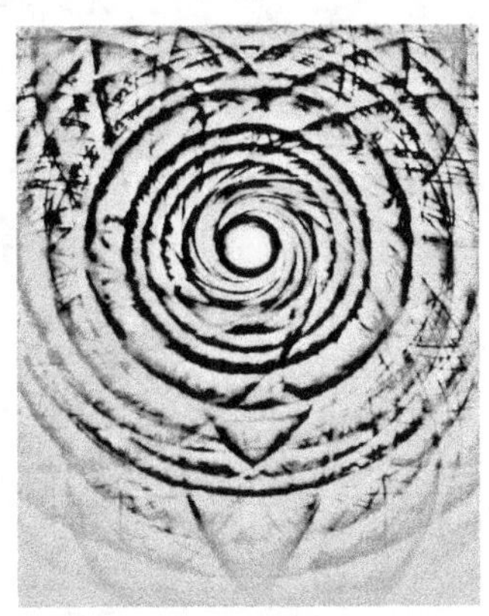

Great News – The Powerful Response to the Challenge

Power of Prayer

As I noted earlier, the power of prayer, both individual and collective, holds the ultimate source of salvation of humankind from the perceived threat of extinction from global climate change.

Children's Near-Death Experiences

I am particularly encouraged by P.M.H. Atwater's observations that we may in fact be witnessing the *birth of a new race of people* on earth who may dramatically impact humankind's rediscovery of spiritual truths.

Greta Thunberg

At age 15, a young Swedish climate activist, Greta Thunberg, began a climate change protest outside the Swedish Parliament in August 2018. Her "school strike for the climate" attracted media attention. From such attention, she has now become a well-known outspoken climate activist. The school strike for climate movement began in November 2018 and spread globally after the United Nations Climate Change Conference in December of the same year.

On March 15, 2019, an estimated 1.4 million students in 112 countries around the world joined her in striking and protesting. A few weeks later, on May 24, 2019, students in 125 countries staged similar events.

As a result of her actions, Thunberg has received various prizes and awards for activism. In fact, in March of that year, three members of the Norwegian Parliament nominated her for the Nobel Peace Prize. At age 16, she was featured on the cover of *Time* magazine. The impact of her actions is now referred to as the "Greta Thunberg effect."

The Sunrise Movement

An American youth-led political movement led by the non-profit organization *Sunrise* advocates for political action on climate change. Incorporated in 2017, the group's goal was to elect proponents of renewable energy in the 2018 midterm elections, first in the Democratic Party primaries, and then in the general election. Following the election, the organization has focused on gaining consensus within the Democratic Party, and being supportive of the environmental program known as the Green New Deal.

On January 2014, The US Climate Plan was incorporated as a nonprofit organization (a.k.a. Sunrise Movement Education Fund). This incorporation was the result of actions taken in the summer of 2013 when Evan Weber, Matthew Lichtash and Michael K. Dorsey used a $30,000 grant and free office space provided by the Sierra Club and the Wesleyan University Green Fund to draft ambitious plan for climate action.

In 2019, climate change action became a major issue for many of the Democratic Party nominees for President.

Green New Deal (GND)

Recognizing the connection between climate change and economic inequality, in the 116th session of the United States Congress, House Resolution 109, sponsored by Representative Alexandria Ocasio-Cortez (D-NY) and Senate Resolution 59, sponsored by Sen. Ed Markey (D-MA), were introduced. The GND refers back to the **New Deal**, a set of social and economic reforms and public works projects undertaken by President Franklin D. Roosevelt in response to the Great Depression. Both lawmakers released a 14-page resolution on February 7, 2019 that calls for a "10-year national mobilization." This program seeks to combine Roosevelt's economic approach with modern ideas such as renewable energy and resource efficiency.

Precedent for this plan was set in 2006 by a Green New Deal created by the Green New Deal Task Force as a plan for 100% clean renewable energy by 2030 utilizing a carbon tax, a jobs guarantee, free college, and a single-payer healthcare plan, with a focus on using public programs.

Additionally, in January 2007, journalist Thomas Friedman argued in favor of a "Green New Deal" in the *New York Times* newspaper and *New York Times* magazine. Subsequently, the idea was taken up in Britain by the Green New Deal Group which published its report on July 21, 2008. The United Nations Environmental Programme (UNEP) further popularized the idea when they began to promote it.

As with any new program, only with high-level dedication, energy political savvy, and philosophical vision will the GND succeed.

A Businessman's Response

It is not just our youth that are taking action regarding climate change. Bill Gates, the founder of Microsoft and the second wealthiest man in the world, is taking action against climate change by authoring a forthcoming book "How to Avoid a Climate Disaster," to be published by Doubleday in June 2020.

Gates put his money where his mouth is so to speak when he announced at the United Nations Climate Action Summit in September 2019 that his foundation was working with the World Bank and some European governments to provide $790 million to help millions of the world's small farmers adapt to climate change.

As a very successful entrepreneur, Gates sees the need for the world to *transition to clean electricity.* We can do so in three key ways.

First, *improved energy storage systems.* As an entrepreneur, he has become an investor in a group called Breakthrough

Energy Ventures (BEV). The group invests in a number of companies exploring ways to store energy such as Hydro, batteries, thermal storage, and zero-carbon fuels.

Second, *carbon capture and storage and nuclear.* Gates questions whether lower-cost solar and wind power, along with emerging breakthroughs in energy storage, means that these sources will be enough to get us to carbon-free power grid. He believes, however, that the world must balance the need to eliminate carbon emissions with economic growth. In doing so, we need to consider what solutions would be most affordable.

Gates cites a November 2018 study from researchers at the Massachusetts Institute of Technology (MIT) that found:

- firm low-carbon resources consistently lower decarbonized electricity systems cost

- availability of firm low-carbon resources reduces costs 10% to 60% in zero-CO2 cases

- without these resources, electricity costs rise rapidly as CO2 limits near zero

- batteries and demand flexibility do not substitute for firm low-carbon resources

For a more in-depth look at how Bill Gates is combating climate change, read his website
www.gatesnotes.com/Energy/A-critical-step-to-reduce-climate-change.

A Prince's Response

In Europe, on September 5, 2019, **Britain's Prince Harry** announced the creation of **Travalyst,** an ambitious travel sustainability initiative in partnership with key travel providers. His partners include booking.com; TravelAdvisor; Visa; China's largest travel company—Ctrip; and the Ctrip-owned fare aggregator Skyscanner.

Prince Harry's long-term objective is focused on tackling the travel industry's impact on climate change, improved wildlife conservation, and protecting the environment in top tourist spots around the world. It aims to increase the amount of tourist dollars that go to local communities and finances eco-tourism.

For more details, read www.associatedpress.com/Prince'stravel-project-eco-minded. September 5, 2019.

With the efforts of these two high-profile individuals, we are witness to the growing global awareness of the efforts by a growing number of major world players to combat global climate change.

Phoenix Generation

Kingsley L. Dennis in his book *The Phoenix Generation,* Watkins Publishing, 2014 quotes the famed futurist Buckminster Fuller, "Dear reader, traditional human power structures in the reign of darkness are about to be rendered obsolete–let me expand upon the above opening quote by adding that this obsolescence of the old will usher in the unexpected, unprecedented, and spectacularly new. I'm not talking about a period of rejuvenation, as this suggests a renovation of incumbent systems. I'm speaking in terms of new forms, new arrangements, new structures, new perspectives and new emerging states of *being*. It's about time we stop talking about the 'end of things,' and instead focus our energies on creating and fulfilling our positive, potential futures."

Mr. Kingsley adds that, "We are, quite literally, shifting from one set of C-values: **competition-conflict-control-censorship** to a new set: **connection-communication-consciousness-compassion.** The shift in value systems is being initiated through a confluence of energies that are emerging through people and entering into the world. He goes on to say that, "on a personal level, we are literally being tested as to our world views, values, perceptions and sense of meaning and well-being." That "this new Renaissance is *not emerging from the center*–where the incumbent power structures are strongest–but instead *rising from the periphery*, this gradual formal replacement (or takeover) is actually a better model for social transition."

"One reason is that it avoids a head-on conflict with existing power structures-it *out-takes* rather than *out-fights* the old. This is a more psychologically balanced process as it allows time for people to adapt to the changing social environment – and this is an important concept."

For those who are historically aware, you saw the emergence of this new values program in the *Occupy Wall Street* movement a few years ago. You can also see this emergence in those young people who were fully, deeply and enthusiastically involved in the 2016 campaign of Senator Bernie Sanders for President of the United States. This new generation is now in its preliminary learning stages politically and shows no sign of going away.

Drawing upon the natural compassionate innate goodness of human beings, I see this new generation adopting the **Diamond Principle of Ethical Reciprocity** as its *modus operandi*. Just think how powerful a change that generation might make by combining the wisdom of older generations and the energy and passion of the millennial's of the Sanders generation. This powerful combination can (and undoubtedly will) literally change the world. Older generations (presumably wiser) can aid this by giving guidance and adding wisdom while working with them to obtain success.

Celtic Christianity-Pelagius and Near-Death Experience Wisdom

Several years ago while researching the history of the concept of Original Sin, I became acquainted with British Celtic monk Pelagius. Led by divine guidance, I recently came upon a book entitled *Listening for the Heartbeat of God: A Celtic Spirituality* by J. Philip Newell, Paulist Press, 1997. As I am of 75% Celtic blood, born and raised in the woodlands of central New York State, and a nondenominational ordained minister, Mr. Newell's writings struck a deep, very comforting note within my soul. I hope it will for you also.

Pelagius was born into the Celtic culture in the latter half of the fourth century CE. An ascetic practicing severe self-denial, he is described as being a man of large stature, exuding an enthusiastic view of life and a good teacher.

Reviewing his philosophy of life, I found many areas that could be considered in strong alignment with what many NDE witnesses have reported.

Pelagius in Early Celtic Christianity

Pelagius had a strong sense of goodness in the whole of creation; he saw God's image and spirit revealed in both man and nature. He thought that every child is conceived and born into the image of God. Each newborn comes forth from God containing the original unsullied goodness of creation; saw in each newborn humanities essential blessedness. Creation is essentially good and that the sexual dimension of procreation is God-given. (Motivated by the powerful emotional drive of *re*creation to facilitate and ensure the basic natural process of *re*creation.)

He denied that humans are born depraved, and strongly rejected the philosophy of Augustine of Hippo that man is born depraved. He thoroughly rejected the concept of Original Sin. Pelagius did not deny the existence of evil; just the philosophy that we are bound by our nature to commit evil actions. He likened the concept of evil to that of a fog that blinds us to our true selves. Through the Grace of Wisdom, we have free will to express our inborn God-like goodness.

In the British Celtic reverence for nature, he saw a sense of stewardship; he read into Jesus' commandment to love not only our neighbors but all the life forms surrounding us. He saw the image of God in everything.

Pelagius understood redemption in terms of free will, setting us free; releasing us of what we essentially are. Planted within us by God, redemption only awaits release. Christ's teaching brings each person liberation, a freeing of the goodness within us which is at the very heart of life. If we desire to find the light by which to live, we need only to look into our own hearts. He believed our deepest desires are to know God and for what is good.

Typical of early British cultural norms and the British church, he supported teaching women to read Scripture, that they were nurtured and freed by the Grace of Wisdom.

Of great importance to Pelagius was that Jesus' basic teaching was entirely concerned with action and with the motives which inspired that action. He contrasted those of Christians who worship daily but performed no good actions with those who did good but did not claim to be Christians, and asked which one better fulfills Jesus's teaching to serve others.

Pelagius believed that the ministry of the church is to liberate and free the goodness of God that is already at the very heart of all life. The gift of the gospel is that we are instructed by Grace of Christ to show the goodness of God within us all.

His philosophy stressed that wisdom consists of listening to the commandments of God written into our hearts and obeying them. A person who has heard that God commands people to be generous and then shares what he has with the poor is truly wise. A person who has heard that God commands people to forgive, and then reaches out with love to his persecutors, is truly wise.

Near-Death Experience – Complementary Wisdom

Many NDE witnesses reported that the nature of God is pure love, appears as energy or light of any shape, is unconditionally loving, forgiving, compassionate, non-judgmental, is neither male nor female, infinite, a part of everything that exists, grants and respects free will, and has a great sense of humor. This sounds like God the Pelagius believed in and was the animating creative force of all that exists.

Love is the true religion. God is love thus love is supreme. Because we are an intimate creation of God-love; we are innately good.

The purpose of life is to become more God-like, to love and forgive unconditionally with compassion for all, and to serve others without concern for a personal reward; selfless service to others.

One consistent element of an NDE is a life review; a panoramic review of the life they just lived from birth to death or in reverse order. They sometimes relived their past, rather than dispassionately viewing it. The greatest impact of this review comes from experiencing the results of our actions as felt from the views of others, the full power and impact of the choices we made; what many people call a celestial "timeout." In essence, they get an interim "cosmic report card," self-scored, an opportunity to return, to try to make amends for past errors, and resolve to live life with more love and joy. This life review thus amply demonstrates the doctrine of *power of free will* to save our lives, ourselves, that Pelagius so strongly believed in.

Our actions and motives are central to our own salvation. It is the *spiritual condition of our heart* that matters most. We ascend to the energy level in the afterlife that our energy, our actions on earth generated. How well did you love?

An Alternative Spiritual Expression?

It would seem at this point in time that we are indeed at a virtual spiritual crossroads. With all the good positive news being brought to us by survivors of the near-death experience and all the not-so-good news about the global climate crisis we face, it appears that mankind could learn much from the positive empowering philosophy of Pelagius; providing a sound theological basis for affirmative climate control measures and actions. What we may, in fact, have in Pelagius is a *Patron Saint for the Earth!*

With almost 23% of Americans expressing no religious affiliation and many mainline churches hemorrhaging membership, it's obvious that many Americans, especially millennials, are looking for an alternative to the religious culture into which they were born and raised.

Combining the positive messages being brought to us by near-death experiencers and the affirming ancient wisdom philosophy of Pelagius, humankind could perhaps even discover the form of a new spiritual/ religious expression.

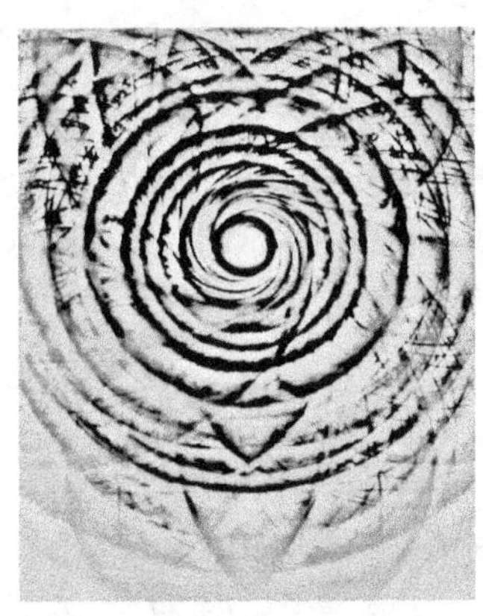

Supporting Research

A Joyous Journey

For readers who may not be familiar with the NDE phenomena, I offer in the following description the common elements of the near-death experience and some of the gifts of wisdom gained by survivors. While each report from individual survivors is unique to their own journey, there are *several common elements* to the vast number of reported near-death experiences.

World renowned authority on NDEs P.M.H. Atwater, author of *Coming Back to Life, Beyond the Light* and several other books, experienced three NDEs in 1977. Drawing on her four decades of experience, she describes an NDE below. I've added to her description other observations offered by the International Association for Near Death Studies, Inc. (IANDS) and Kevin Williams at www.near-death.com. My own comments are in *italics*.

Dr. Atwater begins with:

- A sensation of floating out of one's body. Often followed by an out-of-body experience where all that goes on around the "vacated" party is both seen and heard accurately.

Verifiable information has been presented by many NDErs. For instance, when a person is clinically dead (no heartbeat and with their brain flat-lined), they can describe in detail the actions and communication of medical staff attempting to resuscitate them.

Other reports begin similarly with an awareness of being dead and the experience of leaving their bodies and entering a place of pure darkness which some call *The Void*. For the vast number of persons who have been here, this is a pleasant place. Only about 1% report this being a hellish place where the denizens of this plane seem trapped in repeatedly experiencing their present life void of love or care for anyone other than themselves. How long they stay in *The Void* depends upon the NDErs own belief systems. For those souls who have inflicted much pain and sorrow upon huge numbers of others, they may remain here for an extended period of time—decades or even centuries measured in earth time—until they show a willingness to see the light, experience love for others, and to receive God's forgiveness.

While in the void, many report seeing Beings of Light (some people refer to these as Angels) nearby and available to assist them to learn the reality of eternal love and forgiveness.

Overall, most people stay there just long enough to get oriented to this new realm of existence.

There is hope for us all. We attain the level we set for ourselves in this lifetime. That we have the power to move on to higher levels I find personally reassuring.

The laws of quantum physics tell us that everything is in constant flux; nothing stays the same forever. That's why, in my opinion, the doctrine of eternal hell is misleading. People who find themselves in an unpleasant hellish-like experience have found they do continue to evolve spiritually, albeit slowly; as a result, they are not left there throughout eternity. There is hope for forgiveness and redemption for even in the most morally-depraved persons. If they don't go to heaven, then none of us do. It's an all-or-nothing experience.

- Passing through a dark tunnel, a black hole or encountering some kind of darkness. This is often accompanied by a feeling or sensation of movement or exhilaration. "Wind" may be heard or felt.

- They exit the tunnel into a place of light; filled with dazzling color, a celestial landscape in a different, unearthly world where all objects seem to be composed of shimmering energy. This is a light of incredible brilliance, not blinding nor unpleasant to the eye. Some report seeing people, animals, plants, lush outdoors, and even cities within the light.

I suspect that such familiar scenes may provide these witnesses with familiar psychological reference points in order to provide a sense of comfort as they initially orient themselves to their new experience.

- While their thought processes speed up, time seems to either speed up or slow down. They get a feeling of happiness or joy; a sense of harmony, of unity with the universe.

- Being greeted by friendly voices, people or beings who may be strangers, loved ones, or religious figures such as Jesus. They may feel a presence, or hear an unidentifiable voice.

Conversation can ensue; information or messages may be given. Survivors like Mellen-Thomas Benedict received important scientific information that led him to obtain *patents on new medical technology.*

The communication they engage in may be with a celestial light or Beings of Light (some call Angels). Their senses feel more vivid, experiencing feelings of peace or pleasantness. They are aware of things going on around them, as if by extrasensory perception (ESP).

Unconstrained by the mechanics of our physical communication system, they are part of the Universal Mind and thus communicate directly from one mind of consciousness to another.

- A warped sense of time and space. Witnesses discover that time and space do not exist, they lose the need to recognize measurements of life as either valid or necessary.

- Seeing a panoramic review of the life they lived, from birth to death or in reverse order, sometimes a reliving of their present life rather than a dispassionate viewing. The person's life can be reviewed in its entirely or in segments. The greatest impact of this review comes from experiencing the results of their actions as felt from the view of others.

We feel their joy and their pain, the full power and impact of the choices we made.

In accord with the universal law of human behavior, the Diamond Principle of Ethical Reciprocity, previously referred to, they experience what many people call a celestial "time out." The feelings they experience are seen as an opportunity to review their present life's "successes and failures" as a chance to learn from their mistakes and to make major course corrections in their life before returning to "The Other Side". They may also see scenes from the future, or gain sudden insights or understandings.

In an effort to help us cope with this situation, Beings of Light can take part in this self-judgment-like process and offer escape advice.

I find it comforting knowing that we are never totally alone.

In essence, they get an interim Cosmic Report Card, self-scored, giving them the opportunity to return and make significant journey course corrections.

- They then experience coming to a border, a place of no return. At this point they may still feel connected to the physical body by a "silver cord." If they choose to stay, the silver cord is cut and the option to return to this earthly plane is no longer available.

- Disappointment at being revived. They may experience such pure joy in this advanced realm of existence that they are reluctant to return; often feeling a need to shrink or somehow squeeze back into their physical body. There can be unpleasantness, even anger or tears at the realization they are now back in their bodies and no longer on "The Other Side."

They realize either their job on earth is not finished or they must have a mission yet to be accomplished before they can return to stay.

I had a friend who clinically died, experienced an NDE, was revived, and returned very agitated. "Why the hell didn't you just leave me there? I was happy, I didn't want to come back."

To prevent that from happening again, he posted a Do Not Resuscitate policy notice to his family, friends and medical support. To further ensure non-resuscitation, he apparently chose to pass over alone in the early morning hours during his sleep. When he ultimately made his transition, I am quite certain he was finally a very happy soul!

Aftereffects

Dr. Atwater reports that about 80% of the people who experienced near-death states claim that their lives were forever changed by what happened to them. Looking more deeply, *a pattern* of surprising dimensions *emerged*. More than just a renewed zest for life, they experienced specific psychological and physiological changes like they have never experienced before.

According to Atwater, the aftereffects resulting from NDEs are numerous, both positive and negative. These experiences alter some lives quite significantly.

One effect most commonly noted is the revelatory nature of the experience. Atwater says, "Most near-death survivors say they don't *think* there is a God, they *know*." The great majority of people who have a near-death experience report that they *no longer fear death.*

Only 21% of persons interviewed by Atwater denied the existence of aftereffects, while 19% claim their lives were radically turned around. It seems to take about *seven years* for most experiencers *to integrate* the aftereffects. Lengthy bouts with depression are not uncommon. They have changed so much that loved ones no longer recognize them, thus divorces are not uncommon, an estimated 80% within 10 years.

Psychological Aftereffects

There seems to be a universal pattern of *seven major elements* in experiencing an NDE.

- **Unconditional love**. Perhaps the most profound change for these witnesses is perceiving themselves as equally and fully loving others, no matter who they are or their circumstances in life. The sudden shift in behavior can be very confusing for family members. In general, this may account for the high divorce rate.

- **Lack of boundaries**. Being wholly loving, they become more playful, more childlike. They also become more trusting of others; on occasion becoming targets for scam artists.

- **Timelessness**. Most begin to "flow" with natural time; clocks and schedules are more meaningless, which can cause major disruptions in the workplace. They are more focused on what is going on in their experience. Thinking hazily, they seem distracted as they re-adjust to the demands of their daily routines.

- **Psychic powers**. Extrasensory perception (ESP) and various types of psychic phenomena become normal and ordinary in their lives. This can really frighten the unprepared and may become misconstrued as "doing the devil's work" when in reality, it's more like they are received "gifts of the spirit." They experience increased *intuitive/psychic* abilities plus the ability to know or "re-live" the future.

- **Reality switches**. Hard-driving "A" types become more easy-going philosophers, while the more laid-back warriors become more energetic "movers and shakers" determined to make a difference in the world.

- **The soul as Self**. They come to see themselves as possessing an immortal soul, a resident in material form on the physical plane. They perceive their body more like a "jacket" that they wear and discard upon physical death. They appreciate the future, thus, the majority accept reincarnation as being valid.

- **Modes of communication**. Atwater reports that for many what was once foreign becomes familiar, and the once-familiar becomes foreign.

They begin to think more abstractly, in grandiose terms, using language in new ways, even developing whole new vocabularies.

Taking into account all the above, some *family relatives share* the positive benefits of the event. On the other hand, the responses of some families is very confusing, thus quite negative, resulting in separation or divorce.

Brain Shift

Perhaps the most important psychological result of an NDE is the ***brain shift in consciousness,*** this results in survivors being *more intelligent and loving* than before; becoming detached from the previous norms with more abstract thinking and the ability to envision broader perspectives for a more compassionate positive life. They access latent talents and, in some cases, display the flowering of genius.

Additional brain-shift factors include:

- being more spiritual and less religious; more philosophical, experiencing various bouts of depression, (resulting apparently from an inability to reconcile the NDE with the reality of their current existence), being more generous and charitable than ever before.

- forming expansive concepts of love, being convinced that their life has a purpose, experiencing child-like sense of wonder and joy, and coming to love and accept others as they are, seeing their full potential.

You can read more about the concept of brain shift by reading Atwater's book ***Future Memory,*** hardcover Birch Lane Press, New York City 1995. I also recommend that you read more about this on her website: www.pmhatwater.com

Physiological aftereffects are also quite astounding. In addition to the above psychological aftereffects, NDEers experience altered energy levels, hypersensitivity to light and sound, lower blood pressure, increased intelligence, find stress easier to handle, and many similar effects.

Atwater reports that 73% of her research base reported incidents of electrical sensitivity. 85% report half of the episode was filled with bright, all-consuming light. 52% reported merging into and joining as one with the light (Being of Light). 80% became unusually sensitive to physical light.

Additionally, some of the major *physiological changes* include:

- Sensitivity to light and sound, avoiding "hard" rock music, preferring classical melodic or natural sounds and become passionate about using music.

- Energy surges up and down the body accompanied by "lights" in the air. Some researchers regard this to be release of "kundalini" energy, though this connection has not yet been scientifically established.

- Electrical sensitivity whereby individuals affect nearby electrical equipment and technological devices.

- Physical differences, along with internal changes, eventually led experiencers to alter their approach to health and healing, employment, finances, lifestyle and relationship issues. To some it felt like they had to relearn how to use their body and brain.

Once adjustments are made, the majority can live healthy, productive lives that are happier, more spiritually-oriented and more energetic than before. To deny or repress the aftereffects seems to leave individuals feeling somehow "incomplete" and can foster unwanted "breakthroughs" years later.

For a small number, not all after-effects are of a positive nature. Researchers report personality changes that lead to distress, psychosocial, or psychospiritual challenges. NDEers may have difficulty integrating their near-death experience into their ordinary daily life.

Their greatest desire is to be a conduit of universal love. This can become confusing for family members who see this sudden switch as being oddly threatening and mistake this "unconditional" way of expressing joy and affection heart-centered rather than person-centered, as being flirtatiously disloyalty. This may account for the divorce rates of 80% within 10 years, as mentioned earlier.

Scientific Evidence Supporting
the Near-Death Experience

As the ancient Greek philosopher Heraclitus observed, "All is flux, nothing stays still" and "There is nothing permanent except change." From the world of quantum physics, we see that everything is interconnected by quantum consciousness. At the atomic level, everything is in constant motion.

The Judeo-Christian Bible declares that it all began when God said, "Let there be light." Many of the world's most ancient religious texts associate light with divine consciousness from which everything, including all consciousness, originates.

Physicists such as David Bohm considered all matter to be "condensed" or "frozen light." Others like Stephen Hawking believed that when you break down atomic particles to the most elemental level, you are left with only pure light. The recent discovery of the Higgs particle (the so-called "God particle") has provided evidence of the basic mass from which all other particles are created. Albert Einstein's famous E = MC^2 (E= energy, M= mass, and C = the speed of light squared) mathematically expresses the phenomenal power and energy holding all atoms together.

Verifiable Evidence

Having discovered books on quantum physics and the near-death experience in 1978, pioneering in the field of environmental impact analysis and a university instructor of environmental studies at three universities, I have been trained to *prove it!*

In our materialistic-intellectually oriented world, the scientific community demands that any phenomenon be verifiable. If it cannot survive rigorous test to rule out all of the alternatives (cannot be falsified), it is not to be taken seriously and is dismissed as pseudoscience.

While many skeptical medical researchers still insist that the near-death experience is a result of physiological changes in the human brain, they are not able to explain the *verifiable evidence* acquired during the past 40+ years.

They fail to explain how some persons certified to be "clinically dead" can describe events, some in great detail, in which medical personnel engaged while their brain was certified as being totally nonfunctional, flatlined, and unresponsive.

I present here brief summaries of just a few of the many books and articles presenting provable verifiable evidence for the existence of life after life and the many realms of existence beyond this earthly plane.

Presentation of the phenomena of near-death experiences began with the publication in 1975 of Dr. Raymond Moody's *Life After Life*. His book was followed soon after by the publication of the studies by Dr. Kenneth Ring, Dr. Michael Sabom, P.M.H Atwater, Dr. Bruce Greyson, and numerous others.

An inspirational NDE

Dr. George Ritchie was a private in the U.S. Army in 1943. Suffering from an acute episode of pneumonia, he died, was dead for nine minutes, and then returned. While out of his body, he traveled to a distant location about 523 miles away. He was able to provide solid details of an area he had never been to. Three key aspects of his account have been verified by a third-party, NDE expert Robert Mays (www.subconsciousmind.com).

In 1978, Richie wrote about his NDE in his book *Return From Tomorrow*, Chosen Books, in which he tells about meeting with Jesus Christ, receiving a guided tour of the earth-bound realm, traveling through different dimensions and spaces with Jesus, and his own experience in heaven. He was taken to another realm and shown a kind of "receiving station," a place where people arrived in a deep sleep. Here "Angels" tried to wake them up to the truth that God is truly a God of the living and that they don't have to wait for someone to come and awaken them to the truth of God's love. Further, he describes the horrors of hell, observation of the temple of wisdom, and a heavenly city. He saw governments being torn apart because of *people thinking only of themselves.*

Dr. Ritchie concluded two things; one, that our consciousness does not cease with physical death but, in fact, becomes more keen and aware than ever. Two, how we spend our time on earth and the kinds of relationships we build are vastly more important than we realize.

(His descriptions of the afterlife have been echoed by many others who've undergone a near-death experience).

Later in 1991, he authored his second book, ***Life After Dying: Becoming Alive to Universal Love.*** The main point of this book is to warn us that if we don't let go of earthly bound obsession, they could plague us for the rest of eternity.

It was the transcendental nature of Dr. Ritchie's NDE that inspired Dr. Moody to begin his pioneering studies into the nature of NDEs.

Children's Near-Death Experiences

In her 1999 book ***Children of the New Millennium: Children's Near-Death Experiences and the Evolution of Humankind,*** P.M.H. Atwater presents important information on the near-death experiences of children. She notes that they're not all that different than those of adults. More importantly, these millennial children possess heightened sensory and empathetic abilities acquired at birth or as the result of a near-death experience. This could signify the presence of a *new race of people* on earth and "how these special children will dramatically impact the human condition helping humankind rediscover spiritual truths needed to survive in a radically changing world."

Skeptics are wrong

Jeffrey Long, M. D., a radiation oncologist, in his book, ***Evidence of the Afterlife, the Science of Near-Death Experiences,*** explored nine lines of evidence that he believes provide proof of the reality of near-death experiences. His research, based on over 3,000 near-death experiences, refutes the skeptics who argued that limited brain functioning may explain this phenomenon.

In order to pursue what he believed was proof of the experience, Dr. Long and his wife Jody, established the Near-Death Experience Research Foundation (NDERF) in 1998. Its mission is to research and study consciousness experiences and to spread the message of love, unity and peace around the world. The foundation's website is the world's largest with over 4,600 experiences in 23 languages.

For more information about their work, contact them at: www.nderf.org

We are eternal spiritual beings

The Self Does Not Die: Verified Paranormal Phenomena from Near-Death Experiences, authored by Titus Rivas, Anny Dervin, Rudolph H. Smit, Robert G. Mays and Janice Miner Holden studied over 100 reliable, often first-hand accounts of perceptions, that were later verified by independent sources. They provided evidence that NDEs are not just elaborate hallucinations produced by dying brains nor exuberant fantasies of attention-seeking narcissists. They carefully studied NDEs which occurred during cardiac arrest and other causes and concluded that there are good reasons to assume that our consciousness does not always coincide with the functioning of our brain. Their studies indicate that consciousness can sometimes be experienced separately from the body.

Directions to heaven?

The Map of Heaven, by Dr. Eben Alexander, recalls experiencing an NDE in which the destruction of his neocortex greatly heightened his awareness. He focused on two commonly-witnessed clinical phenomena that defy the simplistic brain-creates-mind model. The first, *Terminal Lucidity* reports that demented elderly patients close to death often experience astonishing cases of recognition, memory, insight, and reflection as they approach death, even being fully aware that departed souls were there to escort them into the spiritual realm.

Secondly, *Acquired Savant Syndromes*, such as experienced in autism, head injury, stroke, or some form of brain damage exhibits some super-human mental capacities such as advanced calculation abilities, intuition, medical abilities, or perfect memory of numbers, names, dates, or visual scenery.

The blind can "see"

Mindsight: Near-Death and Out-of-Body Experiences in the Blind, authored by Dr. Kenneth Ring, investigated the astounding claim that blind persons, including those blind from birth, can actually "see" during near-death or out-of-body experiences. He investigated case histories of blind persons who actually reported visual experiences during an NDE. While the blind do "see," it is not sight as persons with normal visual capacity experience.

It's a sort of "transcendental awareness" referred to as Mindsight, viewing in detail, sometimes from all angles at once, with everything in focus and a sense of knowing the subject, not visually, but with multisensory knowledge.

Does consciousness survive physical death?

Science and the Near-Death Experience: How Consciousness Survives Death by Chris Carter pushes the boundaries further. A belief in an afterlife seems to be fundamental to human experience dating back at least to the Neanderthals. Using scientific evidence, the author challenges materialistic arguments against consciousness surviving death and shows how NDEs may truly provide a glimpse of an awaiting after-life. Reviewing the many psychological and physiological explanations for NDEs (such as birth memories, oxygen starvation or stress) shows how each of them fail to really explain the NDE phenomena.

A new universal science of consciousness?

Dr. Sam Parnia and his co-author Josh Young explored what happens to human consciousness during and after death. Dr. Parnia is founder of the AWARE study (AWareness during REsuscitation) and is one of the world's leading experts in the scientific study of death, the connection between the human mind and brain, and the near-death experiences. Using cutting-edge research, Dr. Parnia believes we are making previously-unthinkable technological progress in our battle against death; that we may inadvertently be discovering a *new universal science of consciousness* that reveals the nature of the mind and the so-called human soul.

Could this be the new children of the Millennial of whom P.M.H. Atwater cited earlier as the future founders of this new universal science?

Self-knowledge is the key

As noted earlier, and worth repeating, over the entrance to the ancient Greek Temple of Apollo at Delphi is written these words, *Know Thyself and thou shalt know all the mysteries of the gods in the universe.* You can ensure entry into a higher realm right now by taking the time to do your own "life review" of your successes and so-called failures. (There is no such thing as a failure, there are no "accidents," only opportunities to learn the lessons we choose to learn in this lifetime.)

Quantum Physics

Science affirms our co-creative power with and from the One Source.

"Quantum physics tells us that nothing that is observed is unaffected by the observer. That statement, from science, holds an enormous and powerful insight. It means that everyone sees a different truth because everyone is creating what they see." Neale Donald Walsch, author *Conversations with God.*

Several prominent members of the scientific community offered the following.

Dr. William Joseph Bray author of *Quantum Physics, Near Death Experiences, Eternal Consciousness, Religion, and The Human Soul,* published in 2012, explains what quantum physics is at its origins and the idea of how our "consciousness paints the universe into being."

Dr. Bray suffers from a condition known as LQT3, a gene mutation which affects the ionic currents in his heart, leading to repeated cardiac arrests. This condition has led him to experience *multiple medically-documented NDEs.* What I found of particular interest is his explanation of how we interact with, manipulate, and define the universe. He believes that his analysis and those of other scientists disprove beyond any reasonable doubt the materialists' claim that consciousness is an artifact of the physical brain.

He concludes that consciousness is a primary entity of our reality. This is the ancient philosophy of Idealism, which had its origins in ancient Greece via the teachings of Plato and Aristotle, later updated by such luminaries as Rene Descartes and Arthur Schopenhauer. Dr. Bray's idea resembles the concept of *panpsychism,* the belief that everything material, however small, has an element of consciousness.

I believe Dr. Bray has been gifted with a personal medical condition that has empowered him to help us bridge the gaps between quantum physics, consciousness, religion and the human soul – a divine gift to humankind.

Dr. Eben Alexander, a prominent neurosurgeon, once thought that he could explain the NDE phenomena as functions of the brain; however, his own NDE during which he was in a coma for seven days completely shifted his view. In 2012, he shared his story in his book *Map of Heaven.*

He states that, "There is no scientific explanation for the fact that while my body lay there, my mind (my conscious inner self) was alive and well. When the neurons of my cortex were stunned to compete with an activity by the bacteria that had attacked them, membrane-free consciousness journeyed to another, larger dimension of the universe—a dimension I've never dreamed existed in which the old, pre-coma me would have been more than happy to explain what was a simple impossibility."

The above description is one of many that suggests that consciousness never ceases to exist. When we die, we leave the body behind, but it doesn't mean we are gone forever. Being out of sight is not the same as being out of mind.

All is mind (the divine law of Oneness) in that the mind never dies–it just experiences different "parts" of itself.

When we die, we simply "shift" to another experience within the one cosmic mind. We are still conscious and aware after we die. We are conscious beings; when the body dies, the consciousness continues.

Gary R Reynard also mentions this in his book *The Disappearance of The Universe.* He says, "What you call this side and the other side are really just two sides of the same illusory coin. It's all universe of perception. When your body appears to stop and die, your mind keeps right on going."

Considering the above studies, to me, religious faith and scientific reason are two complementary languages describing one phenomenon; therefore, I see *no reason not to have faith.*

As Albert Einstein once said, "Science without religion is lame. Religion without science is blind."

Perennial Principles – Universal and Timeless

Witnesses revealed what I believe are *five ancient perennial principles.*

1. There is **One Source** of creation, the One Presence that permeates all of creation; unconditionally loving, forgiving, and compassionate; with a sense of humor. Many people have reported meeting a *Being of Light,* a single entity who expressed unconditional love for them, and also meeting other Light Beings. As a result, many believed that they had met God and Angels.

This Being of Light is known by many names. Persons of western religious faith perceive it as a deity; Yahweh, God, or Allah. In Hinduism, it is Brahman, the *Absolute Principle,* The Atman, the *immanent eternal self.* I choose to refer to it as the **One Source.** *Omnibenevolent*-all good, *omnipresent*-everywhere present, *omniscient*-all-knowing and *omnipotent*-all-powerful.

Persons who employ scientific reason refer to it variously as Ultimate Reality, The Force, (May The Force be with you!), The Field of Infinite Potential, The Singularity, and similar names.

2. There is **One Truth**; manifested as eternal energy which unites all expressions of religious traditions and scientific reasoning. It is based on two principles: *love and wisdom.* All major religions support these two facts, even modern science seems to support it.

The laws of quantum physics reveal that we live in an intimately interconnected, interactive, interdependent, infinite universe. The universe exhibits wholeness, a state of being, an undivided unified whole.

Human beings are part of this creation, connected to all of nature. We are one of the light and darkness, the oceans and the land; the fish, birds and beasts of the earth. We are one with every human being on the planet. Divine intelligence is the foundation of all that is or ever will be; we are one with all.

3. There is **One Consciousness – Universal Mind,** the One Source in action. One of the most common elements reported by these cosmic witnesses is entering into "the void" – a place of complete darkness. As noted above, they met a Being of Light who communicated to them telepathically.

One of the best-known NDE witnesses is Mellen-Thomas Benedict. He referred to the void as being less than nothing, yet more than everything that is. Scientists believe that the void exists in space between individual atoms. They call it the Zero-Point Energy Field. It is a place full of energy, the kind of energy that created everything, the whole of the universe.

Benedict referred to this in biblical terms as "The I Am" with a question mark behind it. "I am? What am I?" He understood the question as being *God exploring God's Self* in every way imaginable; further expressed as an ongoing, infinite exploration of every one of us. His near-death experience brought him to see that everything that is, is the Self; literally, your Self, our Self. Everything is the Great Self. To him, this is why God knows everything. It is therefore possible that wherever we are is a center of the universe, that God is in that place, and more importantly, God is in the void.

Our minds are an intimate part of this great all-knowing Self, thus **we co-create the world in which we live.** It begins with awareness, the capacity to sense and react to various stimuli in the world in which we live. Our challenge is to know *who we are.* As noted earlier, the ancient Greeks counseled us, "Know Thyself and thou shalt know all the mysteries of the gods and the universe."

Historically, the concept of universal mind was originally conceived in ancient Greece by the pre-Socratic philosopher Anaxagoras in his doctrine of *nous* ("mind" or "reason") about 480 BC. He believed the growth of living things depends on the power of the mind within their organisms that enables them to extract nourishment from surrounding substances. However, both Plato and Aristotle objected. In their opinion, his notion of mind did not include the idea that mind also acts ethically (i.e., acts in the "best interests" of the universe).

The concept of Anaxagoras' nous doctrine was further developed and brought forth in 1922 by the French theologian Teilhard de Chardin in his writings on Cosmogenesis in which he introduced his concept of the Noosphere—a third layer of consciousness above and beyond the Geosphere (inanimate matter) and the Biosphere (animate matter). He believed that human activities had created a layer of consciousness that surrounds the earth just beyond the stratosphere. At this level is a record of all the thoughts and events that have ever occurred in the earthly plane since the creation of the earth.

During this same time period, Edgar Cayce, the famed Sleeping Prophet and founder of the Association for Research and Enlightenment (A. R. E.) in 1931, spoke about the *Akashic Records,* or "The Book of Life" in which all the information for every individual who ever lived on the earth is recorded. He also referred to it as God's "book of remembrance." According to A. R. E., these records "contain the entire history of every soul since the dawn of creation. They are a portion of the Divine Mind. They mold and shape levels of human consciousness. They are the unbiased judge and jury that attempt to guide, educate and transform every individual to become the very best she or he can be. They embody an ever-changing fluid array of possible futures that are called into potential as we humans interact and learn from the data that has already been accumulated."

Mr. Cayce discovered that he had the ability to self-induce a sleep-like state that put his mind in contact with all time and space—*the super-conscious* mind. While in this deeply meditative state, he could respond to a variety of questions about the universe, the purpose of life, how to heal ailments specific to an individual, philosophy and reincarnation, dream interpretation, and the ability to read to a person specific sections of their book of life.

As both the Noosphere and the Akashic Record are based in the activities of the human mind, I find that they have a certain amount of parallel wisdom.

A Fourth Level of Existence

I postulate the existence of a fourth level, **The Transphere,** where the patterns of human behavior emerge from the laws of nature, particularly quantum physics. It is here that all the realms of existence beyond the earthly plane (Geosphere, Biosphere, and Noosphere/Akashic Record) are found. This is the source of most ancient wisdom. It is the realm of the super-conscious mind.

Here we find The One Source, God/Ultimate Reality, the One Process of revealing and healing. It is from here that we receive all the wisdom we require to achieve ultimate self-realization on our journey to achieving our maximum spiritual growth. Here are recorded all the lessons in a vast cosmic curriculum, all the lessons that we need to achieve the ultimate realization previously referred to, in particular those tough love lessons—"the traumas of dramas" as I refer to them.

I believe it is from here that humankind gains all of our intuitive insights. We have direct access to them, via our super-conscious mind, through prayer, meditation, and stream of consciousness writing.

4. There is **One Law of Universal Behavior** guiding human social behavior: "Treat, or do not treat others as you would, or would not, be treated." People of faith commonly refer to this as *the Golden Rule* found in many of the major world religions. Secularists refer to it as the *Ethic of Reciprocity*.

Both concepts complement one another, expressing the same energy, so I have combined them into one: the **Diamond Principle of Ethical Reciprocity**. (See Appendix for an in-depth discussion.)

5. There is **One Power – Affirmative Prayer and Patient Meditation.** Affirmative prayer is acknowledging that we already *are* and *have* what we are seeking. It is learning to quiet our busy thinking mind and open ourselves to the intuitive all-inclusive essence of life.

Prayer is a request for assistance from the One Source and meditation is listening for and receiving the answer. To invoke this power, witnesses counsel us to begin by affirming the presence of the One Source unconditionally loving, forgiving, and compassionate. Affirm that the answer is there and begin to live from that knowing.

Express thankfulness for all that you have, fervently believing that your prayers are always answered. The One Source already knows what you need, therefore all you need do is to be clear about what *you* are requesting. Then simply remain silent and patient to receive an answer. Your answer may not come for a while or may come in a form which you might not recognize. Delight in knowing that sometimes the answer may be something even greater than what you requested!

One of the keys of success the witnesses report comes from focusing on *service to others* without concern for what you may receive in return. It is through unconditional loving service to others that our mutual needs are met reciprocally. They assure us that there is no need to worry. While *our* power is very limited, the power of the One Source is *unlimited*. All we need to do is tap into and align with it. Through prayer we ask, knowing that the universe already knows what we need. Affirmative prayer means we create clarity in ourselves as we seek to communicate to our Higher Power (Higher Self). The answers come as we actively engage in a desired outcome. That is, we begin to align ourselves with universal principles. As we do, we begin to attract what we are desiring.

While the prayers of an individual can make a significant impact, the prayers of as few as 10 people can save a city or 20 can save a nation. There is strength in numbers.

This means that by internally feeling the unconditionally-loving power from the One Source, we have a direct impact on the world around us, empowering us to co-create whatever future we desire.

Prayer, meditation, and reflection directly aligns your body, mind and spirit with the One Source, multiplying and maximizing the creative power with which we were born.

Moreover, knowing and understanding the laws of life (a.k.a. Truth) is not enough. We must also live the truth as we know it, guided by the Diamond Principle of Ethical Reciprocity. As revealed in the process of *Life Review*, we get our first interim cosmic report card and clues as to how we live and can further enhance the quality of life we now enjoy; ultimately achieving full self-enlightenment.

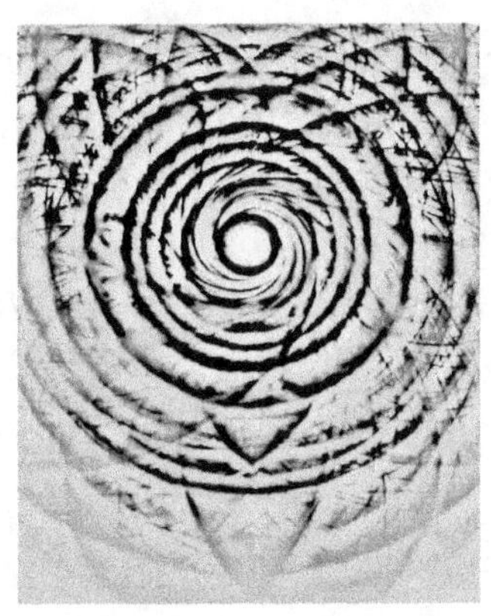

Summary

Overall, what's most important is that *the good news* is comforting, confirming, and empowering.

The Challenging news is frightening in that if we don't act now, our future as a species may be in great danger of self-extinction.

Comforting in that many believe there is a singular source of creation, God. They say, "We no longer *believe* in God, we *know* God exists." They have traveled to other realms of existence beyond this earthly plane (the Void, heaven, hell), report meeting a Being of Light they called God and other beings they call Angels, and have been told that we as God's creation are loved unconditionally and forgiven. Heaven and hell exist but only as states of mind. Eventual escape from hell is assured.

Confirming that we are God's creation, thus we co-create our own world, both individually and cooperatively. Through the power of prayer and meditation we can communicate and align with the power of God. In so doing, we learn our truths, speak them, and act on them.

Confirming in that we have more power than we realize, that many of us, especially our youngest generations, are opening our eyes to the realities of our current global situation and are beginning to take action by either continuing programs already in place or by creating new more powerful ones.

Empowering. The good news is that the future is not fixed and can be changed. The principles of quantum mechanics show that the future is always changing from moment to moment. All of our current actions and decisions directly impact our future. Nothing is absolutely fixed; everything depends on *how we choose to use our free will.* Even those events foretold can be changed or modified by the actions of even one person; like you and me.

In fact, one NDE survivor, Ned Dougherty, was told by a Lady of Light that the world could be saved, not by leaders, but *by prayer groups* throughout the world. A group of 20 could save a nation from war.

The time to act is now!

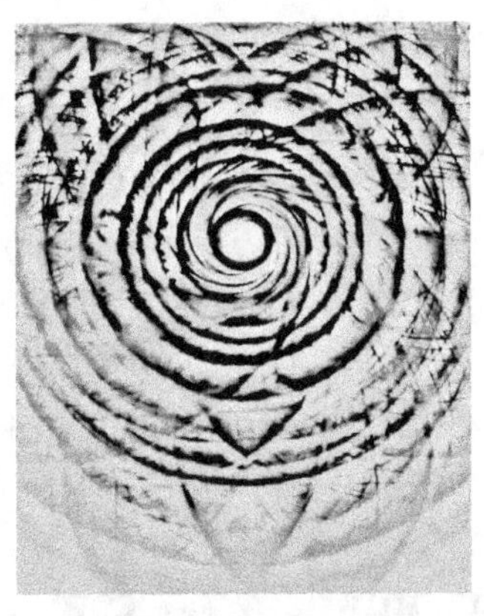

Genius Masterminds:
An Invitation to Have
Some Serious Fun!

As some near-death-experiencers reported, God has a sense of humor; telling some witnesses not to take life so seriously. One witness said that God is a being of pure joy and love with a wonderful sense of humor and an easy ability to laugh.

It is my vision to create a *Genius Masterminds* **team,** a gathering place of seekers-after-universal-truths having some serious fun exploring innovative solutions to current world challenges such as global climate change. While the topics may be of a serious nature, there is no reason not to have some fun along the way. Humorous wordsmithing lightens the emotional aspects and imprints the power of the topics being intellectually researched and presented.

My goal is to:

- Provide *research grants* to minds, young and old, who have the ability to apply the power of *combinatorial creativity:* "the ability to create new combinations from existing resources by recombining ideas, materials and practices, new and potentially unknown possibilities can emerge." (National Science Foundation)

- Attract **genius minds** who combine existing bits of insights, knowledge, ideas, and memories into new material and new interpretations of the world. They can see the seemingly disassociated; see synchronistic patterns where others see only chaos, employing the power of synthesizing mind. Intuitively, they draw upon the collective wisdom of humankind, and often have a "weird" sense of humor. Concisely stated, they are freakin' geniuses!

- Apply the power of a **trans-disciplinary** approach, drawing from a variety of natural (quantum physics, biology, geology and the like) and social sciences (psychology, history, sociology, anthropology, mathematics, and the like).

- Assemble a **multi-generational** team of bright young more technically-skilled minds, experienced middle-years people, and mentored by seasoned elder warriors who together can accelerate the healing process that is so crucial for our human species at the present moment.

Today we live in a world of many global challenges. We are witness to many events both beautiful and horrific due to the internet— mankind's recent gift of global communication.

The internet exposes the great majority of the human family to a wide variety of human actions. Many events in the historical record reveals as having occurred before, in fact many times. History *does repeat* itself over and over.

The Spanish philosopher George Santayana once observed, "Those who cannot remember (or do not know) the past are condemned to repeat it." I expanded the quote by adding *"or do not know"* to more accurately state this human behavioral fact.

The gift the internet now presents us with is a rich store-house of information; both ancient and modern. By remembering, knowing and honestly assessing our history, we can generate insightful energy to avoid repeating those cases where humans have been unimaginably cruel to one another and highlight the many acts of kindness, bravery and generosity seen through history; illustrating the *innate goodness* of all human beings.

- Employ a **trans-cultural** perspective, drawing on the wisdom of Western and Eastern civilizations.

- Employ the most **advanced technologies** to devise new solutions to old seemingly intractable challenges. Persons who possess practical knowledge gained from many years of seasoned experience are particularly and sincerely welcomed.

- **Blend science and spirituality** to see the patterns of human behavior reflected in, and being based upon, the laws of nature, especially in quantum physics.

- Expand **beyond past confining ideologies** and bring forth new solutions to ancient challenges. In the Judeo-

Christian Bible in Ecclesiastes 1:9 we read (paraphrased), "The thing that has been, shall be again; and that which will be done, has been done before. *There is nothing new under the sun.*"

Most new ideas are often created by the synthesizing mind of the creator that see synchronizing patterns. We are often simply reformulating ideas others had set forth many years, or centuries, before.

- Address a wide variety of global and personal issues by applying the power of ***combinatorial creativity*** to combine ancient and modern wisdom with the power of modern technology. It is defined as the ability to "*combine existing bits of insight, knowledge, ideas and memories into new material and new interpretations of the world, to connect the seemingly disconnected, to see patterns rather than chaos.*" *(Maria Popova, smithsonianmag.com June 6, 2012)*

Unity of Opposites

Examples of how these geniuses observe the world can be seen in the notion *of opposites.*

From the field of **quantum physics**, the Principle of Complementarity says that light is both wave-like and particle-like; they are complementary aspects of light.

From the field of **philosophy,** 2500 years ago, the pre-Socratic Greek philosopher Heraclitus of Ephesus, while observing nature, advanced the thesis that the forces of nature are in constant change, "You can never step in the same river twice." He saw that every force in nature is in opposition; one defines the other. For example, hot/cold, up/down, in/out. "The road up and the road down are the same road."

Around the same time, the Chinese philosopher Laozi (Lao Tze), in his famous Dao De Jing (Tao Te Ching) symbol, presents the concept of Yin and Yang, the feminine and masculine, wherein the energy of one is embedded in the energy of the other symbolized by the dot. It is the creative tension between the two that creates beneficial results.

In the field of **psychology**, throughout his writings, Carl Jung notes that there is a continual tension and integration of opposites. Two ideas are presented in opposing pairs in the conscious mind. It is in this creative tension between our conscious and subconscious mind that the archetype is integrated into the self.

The field of **theology**, the sixth century B.C.E. Persian philosopher Zoroaster spoke of the duality of human behavior. He believed that the nature of man is both good and evil, that the human mind is in constant battle between the two.

Further, the 15th century C.E. The Christian philosopher/theologian **Nicholas of Cusa** set forth his concept of **"coincidentia oppositorum";** the holding of two equally valid principles in a state of creative tension that will or can produce a situation he called "dire contradiction." For a person's soul to evolve, they cannot deny the situation. He believed that if a person stays in an emotional state long enough, a third option will occur.

In the field of **economics**, we have Socialism (ownership of all resources are held by the state) and Capitalism (ownership of resources is by individual members of society). In either economic state, we see that in their most extreme control, resources accrue to the benefit of the few as opposed to the needs of the many.

Two Basic Qualities

These genius masterminds have two basic qualities:

1. *Genius is the ability to reduce the complicated to simple.* C. W. Ceran. This is a rare and highly prized gift. With so much data, information, and wisdom available they "cut to the chase" so to speak; separate the wheat from the chaff. Advanced degrees are not a requirement, but may prove to be helpful.

2. *The ability to think outside the box.* These geniuses are natural innovators who employ the power of the synthesizing mind; applying this trans-disciplinary approach to see the big picture and all its ramifications; the forest and the trees and how they interrelate in the natural/ human ecosystem. They see potential solutions where others see intractable problems; connect the seemingly disassociated, see synchronistic patterns where others see only chaos. They do so by drawing upon a wide variety of intellectual and intuitive sources.

Intuitively, they draw upon the collective wisdom of humankind, and often have a "weird" sense of humor. Often considered freaks, they are natural outliers who don't easily fit into neatly defined or confining categories. Free-thinking innovators and inventors, those geniuses who create new ideas and inventions and in the process, break free of stultifying intellectual and emotional constraints. Examples are people like Thomas Edison, Nikola Tesla, Albert Einstein, Elon Musk, Sir Richard Branson, Steve Jobs and Walt Disney.

Outwardly, these geniuses appear to be absent-minded at times, the famous *"absent-minded professor,"* but in reality, they're just distracted by the massive material their synthesizing minds are constantly processing. **Consummate multi-taskers,** concisely stated they are *freakin' geniuses!*

(For an informative and a humorous look at entrepreneurial freaks, read *Freaks Shall Inherit the Earth: Entrepreneurship for Weirdos, Misfits and World Dominators.* Chris Brogan, Wiley and Sons, 2014)

An Invitation to Have Some "Serious Fun!"

- Are you combinatorially creative, a *trans-disciplinarian* skilled at combining existing wisdom into new interpretations, cross-connecting between various disciplines, recognizing patterns among the chaos; *thinking outside of the box?*

- Do you have practical knowledge of particular topics, from the *hard sciences* such as quantum physics, mathematics, biology, or geology and the *social sciences* like history, sociology, political science, anthropology or psychology?

- If you have in-depth knowledge of the world's *major religions* and the teachings, you would serve the team well.

- Are you able to *present your knowledge concisely* (in layman's language) and able to combine science and spirituality, focusing on specific topics?

- Are your intuitive and intellectual capacities well balanced? Do you listen to your own inner voice, your intuition, as it accesses information and use your intellect to organize ("make sense" of) it?

- Do you have an irreverent sense of *humor* and have fun with big ideas?

- Can you "think with your heart and feel with your mind?"

If you said yes to all, or most, of the above, you're invited to *join the Genius Masterminds,* an eclectic group of truth seekers who see the world outside of the box society puts us in; who figuratively speaking, see both the forest and the trees therein, and understand their inter-relatedness.

Utilizing both powers of intuition and intellect, seeing the laws of nature as they appear to influence human behavior, I regard myself as being a "spiritual ecologist," a meta-physician by nature. In fact, this "gathering" is the prime motivation for writing this book. Come on, jump in and enjoy the serious romp!

Let's come together to combine our talents and wisdom to help the world cut through the seemingly endless masses of materials currently circulating in the global community and bring forth golden nuggets of truth, wisdom, and freedom! Employing ancient wisdom from our collective consciousness, let us intuit creative solutions to those familiar old sticky world problems.

Freakin' Geniuses Unite!

If you are combinatorially creative and would like to contribute to this effort, I invite you to contact me at:
www.geniusmasterminds.org

The world needs our genius – now!

Potential Projects

Some of the **potential projects** we might engage in include:

- **The Power of Prayer.** Quantum physics tells us that everything is energy. Thoughts are energy. Harnessing the power of combinatorial creativity would greatly increase the power of prayer. Applying the wisdom gained to creating global prayer power groups would be one very effective method of dealing with current global challenges, especially climate change.

- **Stewardship: Theology of Climate Change.** The wisdom of early Celtic Christian theologians, in particular Pelagius' interpretation of the second commandment which says to love your neighbor *and* their surroundings, provides a good ethical basis for managing climate change. Present-day Celtic religious philosophy is rooted in the ancient Celtic observation that the image of God is everywhere and that humans are intrinsically morally good.

- **The Diamond Principle: Ancient Formula for Lasting Global Peace.** Commonly known as the Golden/Silver Rule combined with the humanists Ethic of Reciprocity, this is as close as a human race has come to creating a universal principle of mutual respect and responsibility. However, for a variety of reasons, it has appeared not to be very successful. Let's explore the many reasons it has not worked and determine how it might. (See *Appendix – Diamond Principle of Ethical Reciprocity* for a more in-depth examination.)

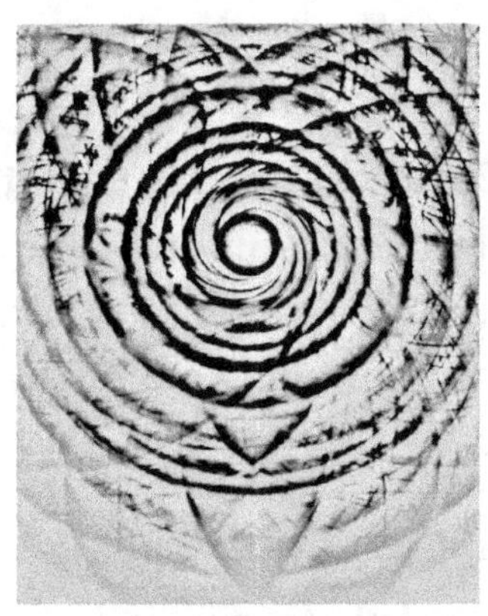

Appendix –
The Diamond Principle
of Ethical Reciprocity

Introduction

Our current global state of affairs is one of a moral crisis brought on by increased ideological conflict that threatens global peace. Is there a God or just a natural force of creation?

One solution may be to re-examine the commonalities between established religions and combine them with modern humanist philosophies. Applying the wisdom of **The Diamond Principle of Ethical Reciprocity** may be an effective avenue to pursue in humankind's ongoing quest for global peace.

Definition

The Diamond Principle is an updated and expanded restatement of the ancient Golden Rule combined with the modern concept of Ethical Reciprocity. It says simply, *"Treat, or do not treat others as you would have them treat, or not treat you, in any given situation."*

Stated in the positive as the "Golden" (do as) and in the negative "Silver" (do not do as), it is found in most major religious philosophies. From ancient Egypt we hear, "Do for one who may do for you, that you may cause him thus to do." *The Tale of the Eloquent Peasant*, 1970-1640 BCE. From the more recent, "He should not wish for others what he does not wish for himself." Baha'i Faith ~1870.[1]

Stated as an ethic, it is found in many humanist writings. For example, "You should always ask yourself what would happen if everyone did what you are doing. " *Jean-Paul Sartre*, French existentialist philosopher. "Treat others as you'd want to be treated in their situation; don't do things you wouldn't want done to you." *British Humanist Association* 1999.[2] The religious principle and the humanist ethic are essentially the same idea; two principles of human behavior combined into one; *The Diamond Principle of Ethical Reciprocity*, originating in the physical world. As such, it appears to be an almost *universal guiding principle for human behavior.*

Principle, Not a Rule

It is stated as a principle, not a rule. Rules state what is legally or procedurally correct, whereas principles state what is morally or intrinsically correct. Rules are imposed by an established authority, while principles are internal motivation to do the right thing by all persons. "A principle motivates you to do the thing that seems good and right. A rule externally compels you, through force, threat, or punishment to do things someone else has deemed good or right." See Sandra Dodd *Living by Principles Instead of by Rules.*[3]

Physical Characteristics of the Diamond

Why the diamond? Diamonds are composed of *carbon*, the sixth most common element in the universe; the third on earth. *It is the basis of life on earth.* The carbon atom is a friendly little fellow, which through the process of *catenation* (linking atoms into longer chains), it freely makes *covalent* bonds (sharing electrons between atoms) with up to four neighboring carbon atoms to form a whole slew of carbon-carbon compounds. It creates such compounds as:

- *ethane* – used in production of natural gas fuel

- toluene – a widely used industrial solvent and in the explosive TNT

- biphenyl – used to manufacture other chemicals and also used as a fungicide

- acetone – used as a solvent (like paint thinner) and to make plastic, fibers, drugs, and other chemicals

- acetonitrile – also used as a solvent, for spinning fiber and in lithium batteries (essential in electric automobiles)

- ethanol – used as a supplement to gasoline and the primary ingredient in alcoholic beverages[4]

Biological Significance

Most importantly, carbon is the *basis of life on earth.* One atom of carbon combined with two atoms of oxygen creates carbon dioxide, the basis of photosynthesis which takes in CO_2 and combines with water (H_2O). That combination produces sugar ($C_6H_{12}O_6$) and oxygen (O_2) as a byproduct. Sugar is then used in cellular respiration which produces lots of energy as a fuel, with CO_2 and H_2O as byproducts, which starts the whole cycle again. (5)

It Just Makes Good Sense to Focus on the Diamond

As diamonds are composed of carbon, the basis of life on earth, they are rare and beautiful; consequently, they are highly prized valuable personal and commercial assets.

Moreover, as they may be the natural basis of compassion as part of *human innate goodness,* it makes good sense to use the carbon-based diamond as the ultimate standard upon which to measure human behavior.

As we move into this fourth level of enhanced human collective consciousness *(The Super-conscious),* the human family has an opportunity to achieve an unprecedented degree of global cooperation. We have reached a place where we can achieve the long sought world peace *if* we effectively apply ancient knowledge.

Attributes

This principle is based on the philosophy of *mutuality,* (a reciprocity of sentiments)[6] our natural state of co-existence, aka *reciprocal benevolence*[7] incorporating a state of *enlightened self-interest.* Spiritually it can be seen in the concept of *reciprocal altruism* (to make a sacrifice with the expectation of future reciprocal reward or to cooperate with another for a self-serving purpose.)[8]

Implementation of mutuality has *five basic* elements.

First, basic *human rights.* This recognizes the ideal of equality between all members of the human family. The Universal Declaration of Human Rights signed in 1948 declares that we have 30 basic rights.[9]

Second, *obligations* to defend the rights of others. As I am obliged to recognize and defend your rights, you are, in turn, obliged to recognize and defend mine. This is in essence a social contract in which two or more parties are bound by agreement of mutual support. If, however, one fails to perform, then all parties are released from the agreement. Either we all are in, or we are all out.

Third, we must *know the impact* of our past actions. We are thus obliged to honestly confront our own truths, individually and as a society.

This addresses the whole notion of self-awareness including our transgressions, conscious and unconscious.

Often, we do not know that we have offended or injured another person. When confronted, we must acknowledge our transgressions, ask for forgiveness, and expect redemption.

If we confront another, we must ask that they listen and hear us and that we forgive them for their perceived transgressions against us. And so doing, we may then expect mutual forgiveness and redemption for our transgressions.

Fourth, we must be able to *imagine the impact* our actions may have on future events and commit ourselves to use the Diamond Principle as a guide to all future actions. Spanish philosopher George Santayana once observed, "Those who cannot remember the past are condemned to repeat it." More accurately it should read, "Those who cannot remember (*or know)* the past are condemned to repeat it."

If we as individuals cannot remember our past actions, we repeat them, repeatedly! It's like trying to move forward with one foot nailed to the ground. We just go 'round and 'round repeating the same mistake. More significantly, if we as a human family do not know our past, it will come back to haunt us like a lost soul looking for redemption.

Fifth, we must apply this principle *fairly and consistently* in all present and future actions. Life is an ongoing process that requires constant daily monitoring.

Each event presents us with an opportunity to deal with life's challenges. As we live our lives, we must constantly be fair in our dealings and apply the Diamond Principle consistently in each moment of our life.

What This Principle Does Not Do

This principle does not involve *tit-for-tat revengeful principles.* The ancient Hammurabi idea of an eye for an eye does nothing more than blind all parties, thus this principle cannot be used for justifying *retributive justice* or *laws of retaliation.* Instead, it requires each person to come to the aid of another, wherever possible.

Nor does it condone the idea that, "The best defense is a good offense."[10] This tactic requires one to attack first, often with great furor, leaving the attacker (if he/she survives the attack) open to focus on counter-attack. It violates the whole principle of treating others fairly and with great concern for the welfare of the other. In contrast, however, this principle *does not prohibit*, in case of an attack, *self-defense*. All it says is, "Treat others in ways they might reasonably expect to be treated." It would be destructively naive to simply allow an attack without taking countering action to preserve our safety and security.[11]

Additionally, this principle incorporates *deontological ethics* (from Greek word *Deon* meaning *obligation*), a theory that holds that decisions should be made solely, or primarily, concerning one's rights and duties. Such theory posits the existence of an *a priori* moral obligation, further suggesting that people ought to live by a set of permanently defined principles that do not change merely because of a change in circumstances.[12]

This theory, in fact, presupposes equality of everyone no matter what their stage in life may be. We have in effect *a social contract*, one that promotes mutual rights and obligations to achieve the highest social good.

Two Basic Needs

Underlying observance of this principle is our two basic needs; *safety* (immediate, short term) and *security* (future, long term). Safety involves being personally safe from attack, having enough food, water and shelter for our immediate needs. Security involves group behavior that provides such things as communal safety, good health, education and religious cooperation.

It could serve as a litmus test of character. On a personal level, it seeks to promote self-preservation, self-protection, self-enhancement, and self-worth, while it recognizes individual uniqueness and provides a natural basis for the emotion of love.

Humans are inherently good; they share resources, and have respect for individual creativity, and assume and ensure equality. In the system of social justice, it promotes forgiveness of transgressions and the ability to redeem oneself from past transgressions. It was this quality that enabled humans to form constructive alliances; families, clans, villages, cities, kingdoms, empires and nations.

From a sectarian/religious viewpoint, this quality promotes a natural state of *innate goodness*. This involves the psychology of giving knowing that you receive more than you give. Sharing is seen as a strength, not a weakness.

A New Code of Morality

From all the above, I see the emergence of a new Code of Morality. One that combines the wisdom of the Golden/Silver rule, "Treat, or do not treat others as you wish, or do not wish to be treated," and the Ethic of Reciprocity, "Treat others only as you consent to being treated in the same situation." Updated and restated, it should now read, "Treat, or do not treat another, as you would wish, or do not wish to be treated, in any given situation."

To apply this, we need:

- Knowledge of what effects our actions have on the lives of others and the ability to imagine, accurately and vividly, ourselves on the receiving end of our actions; to "Walk a mile in another person's moccasins."

It must be applied consistently:

- It doesn't replace regular norms.

- It isn't an infallible guide to right a wrong–it doesn't give all the answers.

- It only prescribes consistency; that our actions are in harmony with our desires and those of others.

- It simply tests our moral coherence.

If we violate this new moral code, we then violate the spirit of fairness and concern that lie at the heart of morality.

Globally, it is a principle well-suited to be a standard for different cultures by which they can resolve conflicts.

Faith-based organizations can play a central role in taking the lead in resetting our global moral code. In our global capitalist system, we can create a moral code for all global stock trading organizations and businesses, one that is a win-win. If we establish a code, publish and distribute it to investment firms, and urge them to adopt it, emphasizing its economic value to them, we can collectively make major changes.

Human innate goodness

As noted earlier, due to its naturally friendly bonding qualities, carbon may constitute a natural bonding pre-disposition underlying the human quality of *innate goodness.*

As the chemical nature of carbon gives it a natural affinity to form chemical bonds, human nature, in a similar way, inspires people to form bonds of friendship and love with others.

Recent scientific studies have shown that *compassion is biologically deeply rooted* in our brain. An experiment conducted at the University of Wisconsin by Jack Nitsche showed that when mothers looked at pictures of babies, not only do they report more feelings of compassion and love, they also demonstrated a unique human activity in the region of the brain associated with positive emotions. This finding suggests that there is a region of the brain tuned to the first object of our compassion – our offspring.

Joshua Greene and Jonathan Cohen of Princeton University conducted a set of studies that found when one subject contemplated harm being done to others, a similar network of regions of their brains are activated. Our children and victims of violence are two very different subjects, yet are united by the similar neurological reactions they provoke. This suggests that innate goodness is a human response embedded in the folds of our brains. Logic tells us this must be essential to the preservation of our species and other animals as well.

James Rilling and Jeffrey Burns at Emory University conducted other research that showed given a chance to help someone else triggers activity in the *caudate nucleus* and *anterior cingulate* portions of the brain that turn on when people receive rewards or experience pleasure. This is a remarkable finding: helping others brings the same pleasure we get from the gratification of personal desire. The brain then seems to be wired to respond to others' suffering and makes us feel good when we can, and do, alleviate that suffering.

It seems that a loose association of glands, organs, and cardiovascular respiratory system known as the *autonomic nervous system* (ANS) plays a primary role in regulating our blood flow and breathing patterns for different kinds of actions. For example, when a person feels threatened, our heart and breathing rates usually increase, preparing us either to confront or flee from the threat, the so-called "fight or flight" response.

When young children and adults feel compassion for others, the notion of compassion is reflected in very real physio-logical changes: our heart rate goes down from base levels which prepares them not to fight or flee, but to approach and soothe.

Additionally, there is *oxytocin,* a hormone in our blood-stream that promotes long-term bonds and commitments. This may account for the overwhelming feeling of warmth and connection we feel towards our offspring or loved ones. Indeed, breastfeeding and massages elevated oxytocin levels in the blood (as does eating chocolate – woo hoo!)

The above information was didactic from a study cited in an article, *The Compassionate Instinct,* by Paul J. Zak, California State University -Berkeley. [13]

Zak found that when people perform behaviors associated with compassion and love such as warm smiles, friendly hand gestures, and affirmative forward liens, their bodies produce more oxytocin. This suggests compassion may be self-perpetuating; it causes a chemical reaction in the body that motivates us to be even more compassionate.

These and other studies that show that compassion is an innate part of human nature. [14]

Economically

Economically the compassionate nature of people is *good for business.* Responding to consumer needs creates new consumer goods and services. It inspires and enables employees to create new ideas, employs the power of *combinatorial creativity,* which applies ancient and current knowledge, combined with modern technology in pursuit of new solutions for current global or personal challenges. *Innovation* is therefore seen as an *investment* with almost *guaranteed results.*

Stewardship of Nature

Mutuality also *promotes stewardship,* the wise use of our earth and all its resources, shared equitably for the benefit of all members of the human family. The impact of human activities over the past two centuries has exploited natural resources, endangering our long-term survival. While creating a greatly improved lifestyle of the human race, it has also created almost incalculable detrimental results.

Now we seem to have, as a species, the ability to change the very climate conditions on the blue global orb we inhabit.

We might in fact be seen by Mother Nature as a cancer, with self-extinction tendencies which may result taking the whole of the global ecosystem with us.

Why Hasn't This Principle Been More Effective?

An article published by the Academic Studies of Religion entitled "Ethics of Reciprocity like the Golden Rule and the Wiccan Rede do not work" cast doubt on the viability of these concepts. The authors note that there is a *high-end* and *low-end*. The author says neither of these work. *The High End: Be Kind to Your Enemies* does not work because being kind to your enemies has ironically led humankind to some of the worst atrocities in history by naïvely following ruthless leaders into barbaric warfare and oppression of helpless people. I suspect that the leaders like Genghis Khan, Adolf Hitler, Joseph Stalin, and the famed pirate Bluebeard may qualify in this category.

The Low-End: Do to Others as They Do to You (Fight Fire with Fire!) naively applied as *ethical reciprocity* has given antagonists free reign to lower moral standards to base levels. These individuals may have a different concept of what constitutes moral behavior, and may in fact be amoral.[15] Sociopathic and psychopathic personalities often recognize only their rights without any concomitant sense of obligation to defend the rights of others.

The Great Wedges: Exclusivity and Intolerance

Exclusivity

Defined as "The state or quality of being exclusive; exclusiveness," a factor may be human's strong tendency to engage in exclusivity, the familiar "We are right, you are wrong and we won't discuss it any further."

Moreover, such groups may claim to have exclusive knowledge (in both religion and science). In so doing, they restrict admission to their group, requiring total acceptance of their beliefs, credos or codes of conduct.

While restricting inclusion, they may tolerate the existence of other groups, respecting others without actively opposing their existence.

Intolerance

Intolerance is defined as a "lack of toleration; unwillingness or refusal to tolerate or respect contrary opinions or beliefs, persons of different races or backgrounds, etc." In their close-mindedness, they may engage in bigoted and/or prejudicial actions, even seeking to destroy opposing groups.

Such closed mindedness has led to wars between "believers and infidels" inflicting an incalculable amount of damage on the human family.

Measures to Make it More Effective

Mutual Self-Enlightenment

The simplistic counter-action to exclusivity and intolerance is to demonstrate to persons who engage in such thinking that the universe is intimately interconnected, interactive and wholly interdependent. Their long-term security depends on the cooperation of others in their society and the human family as a whole; that mutual self-enlightenment is the key to a secure and robust future. Together the result is greater than the sum of their individual energies.

Recognize the factors that create and destroy any human enterprise.

Historians recognize the *major factors that created* the world's great civilizations.

- Learning – The act of acquiring new, or modifying and reinforcing existing, knowledge, behaviors, skills, values, or preferences which may lead to a potential change in synthesizing information, depth of knowledge, attitude or behavior relative to the type and range of experience.

- Invention – A skill which allows players to disassemble items and obtain new materials. These can be used to manufacture newly discovered devices and augment a variety of high-level weapons, medicines, and tools, enhancing them with perks – special rewards that are given to people who have a particular job or belong to a particular group.

- Investment – An act of devoting time, effort, or energy to a particular undertaking with the expectation of a worthwhile result.

- Moral code – A written, formal, and consistent set of rules prescribing righteous behavior, accepted by a person or by a group of people.

- Spreading of the wealth – A sharing of money or good fortune with others.

Factors leading to their *downfall* were:

- Excess ambition – Ambition to an excessive degree, having an overly strong desire for some type of achievement or distinction, as power, honor, fame, or wealth, and an overly strong willingness to strive for its attainment.

- Hubris – Excessive pride or self-confidence displayed as arrogance, conceit, haughtiness, pride, self-importance, egotism, pomposity, or superiority.

- Corruption – A form of dishonest or unethical conduct by a person entrusted with a position of authority, often to acquire personal benefit. Corruption may include many activities including bribery and embezzlement. An illegal act by an officeholder that is directly related to their official duties, and done under cover of law or involves trading and influence.

- Injustice – Being unjust or inequitable; violation of the rights of others; unjust or unfair acts; wrong.

- Cruelty – A callous indifference to or pleasure in causing pain and suffering; behavior that causes pain or suffering to a person or animal. Behavior that causes physical or mental harm to another, whether intentionally or not.

These factors can, in fact, be applied to any human enterprise. Underlying these factors is the pattern of expansion and contractions of free will. If the citizens of a nation, employees of a corporation, faculty of an educational institution, or leaders of any religious institution freely add to and enjoy the results of the creative factors, they will add to and expand the energies of the institution to where they invest their creative energies.

If the leadership of any human enterprise recognize, fully understand and support the creative factors, they will enjoy massive results. If they do not, they do so at their own peril.

Source. The above outline of factors was drawn from *The World's Great Civilizations: The Rise and Fall of Nations, from the Ancient to Today*, Life Inc. Specials 11-2-12, page 13. Definitions from a combination of various on-line sources.

Spiritual Aikido

If there are those who think they cannot see the benefit of mutuality, it is incumbent then for others to *remember the exception for self-defense* from attack physically, mentally and spiritually.

By learning how to practice a spiritual form of Aikido, individuals may preserve a state of safety and security. The literal interpretation of the word *aikido* (ai-ki-do) is the "way of combining forces." It was developed in the 1920s and 1930s by the master Japanese martial artist *Morihei Ueshiba* who sought to combine his martial studies, philosophy, and religious beliefs into one martial art.

Ueshiba's goal was to create an art that practitioners could use to *defend themselves* while also *protecting their attackers* from injury. The techniques he developed consist of centering and turning movements that redirect the momentum of an opponent's attack and throw or create a joint lock that terminates the technique. While defending yourself, Ueshiba thought, we must also *have concern for the well-being* of the attacker and harmlessly redirect the momentum of an opponent's attack.

This concept involves equal treatment, the mutuality of "do no harm as you would not be harmed." It uses their momentum against the intent of the attacker to redirect energies into a productive outcome.[16]

Common Ground?

The third element of the Diamond Principle says we must *know the results of our past actions.* This requires us to look honestly at our past actions and to "own" them. The central operative concept here is *empathy;* the ability of people to see and feel the world from the eyes of other persons, enlightening us to their unique worldview. The key is to *empathetically listen*, really listen; hearing from your heart what the other person is saying and sharing, and not just waiting to make your next point.

In the religious world of Christianity, the Lord's Prayer requires adherents to "Forgive us our transgressions as we forgive the transgressions of others." It begins with us, personally and socially.

An Organic Social Contract

Why do I propose the Diamond Principle of Ethical Reciprocity? The carbon element is the basis of life on earth, and natural organic creator. The carbon atom makes atoms into longer chains, sharing items with four neighboring atoms to produce carbon-carbon compounds. It adapts to new conditions, adapts to changes, and mutates into new entities - it evolves!

It is a principle, not a rule. Rules are externally imposed, rigid and inflexible, created closed systems thinking. Principles are internally flexible which like the carbon atom, can adapt to new conditions, and adopt the changes, creating an open system.

Being a principle, individuals are internally motivated to do the right thing by all by based on what is morally and intrinsically correct. Principles therefore transcend the usual limits and transform into new adaptable conditions creating an improved code of human behavior.

Applying the ancient Greek concept of *Unity of Opposites* wherein the *negentropic* force builds, creates order out of chaos, and the opposing force of *entropy* dissipates and decreases order. We can employ their pull-push interaction, manifest energy in new forms, and adapt and adopt the constant flux of energy to mutate and evolve. Together, they create an evolved code of morality, an organic social contract, adopting ancient wisdom while using modern technology to adapt to current world conditions.

In employing the wisdom of the Diamond Principle of Ethical Reciprocity, we emphasize its universality. In the natural world, we see that it is based on the carbon atom, and in the human world, an updated version with the ancient Golden/Silver Rule coupled with the modern Ethic of Reciprocity.

Using the perspective of combinatorial creativity – a multi-disciplinary approach to problem-solving – we can marry ancient wisdom and modern technology to explore new solutions to current world problems.

One good example might be, in the near future, we will see the creation of the *quantum computer*. This new technology can quickly scan and analyze vast amounts of information creating Artificial Intelligence (AI) that can create a vastly improved organic-based code of morality. Programming these powerful tools with the results of recent studies of human nature's *innate goodness*, we can create a vastly expanded code of human interaction, finding commonalities which unites, and attests to our innate natural goodness.

Using the principle of *Spiritual Aikido,* we can redirect counterproductive energies by appealing to the enlightened self-interest and self-preservation of individuals, recognizing that we live in an organic intimately interactive, intercon-nected, interdependent, infinite universe.

A small dedicated group of trans-disciplinary individuals can create such a new code of human conduct via the Diamond Principle of Ethical Reciprocity. See **Genius Masterminds.**

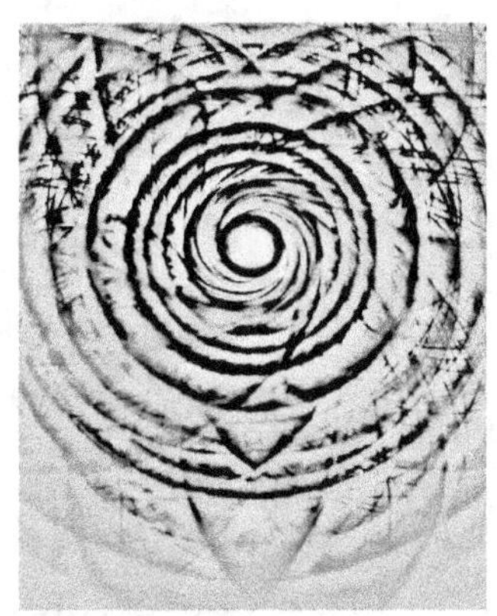

Appendix – References

1. *A humanist perspective on...the 'Golden Rule'*
British Humanist Association 1999 info@humanism.org.uk

2. ibid

3. Sandra Dodd Living by Principle Instead of Rules
http://sandradodd.com/rule

4. *www.pubchem.ncbi.nlm.gov/compounds*

5. ibid

6. *Mutuality* – Thesaurus- noun1.
https://www.thefreedictionary.com/mutuality

7. www.google.com/search=reciprocal+benevolence

8. reciprocal altruism, cooperative egoism Psychology
www.wikia.com/wiki/Ethic_of_reciprocity p.3

9. *Universal Declaration of Human Rights* www.amnestyusa.research/human-rights-basic

10._en.wikipedia.org/wiki/The_best_defense_is_a_good_offense

11. *Ethic of Reciprocity* Psychology. wikia.com/wiki/Ethic_of_reciprocity p.5

12. en.wikipedia.org/wiki/deontological_ethics

13. Jack Nitsche, Joshua Greene & Jonathan Cohen, James Rilling & Jeffery Cohen. All referenced in *The Compassionate Instinct* Paul J. Zak www.greatergood.berkeley.edu

14. ibid

15. *"Ethics of Reciprocity like the Golden Rule and Wiccan Rede do not work."* Academic Studies of Religion www.humanreligion.info/golden.

16. *Aikido www.crakido.com*